Southern Living.
ORGANIZING
made easy

Oxmoor House.

Southern Living.

ORGANIZING
made easy

Created exclusively for *Southern Living At HOME*®, the Direct Selling Company of Southern Progress Corporation.

For information about *Southern Living At HOME*® please write to:
  Consultant Support
  P.O. Box 830951
  Birmingham, Alabama 35282-8451

ISBN: 0-8487-3123-9
Printed in the United States of America
Fourth Printing 2007

Oxmoor House, Inc.
EDITOR IN CHIEF: Nancy Fitzpatrick Wyatt
EXECUTIVE EDITOR: Susan Carlisle Payne
COPY CHIEF: Allison Long Lowery

Southern Living At HOME®
SENIOR VICE PRESIDENT AND EXECUTIVE
    DIRECTOR: Dianne Mooney

Organizing Made Easy

EDITOR: Susan Hernandez Ray
SENIOR DESIGNER: Emily Albright Parrish
COPY EDITOR: L. Amanda Owens
EDITORIAL ASSISTANTS: Shannon Friedmann,
    Brigette Gaucher
DIRECTOR OF PRODUCTION: Laura Lockhart
PRODUCTION MANAGER: Greg A. Amason
PRODUCTION ASSISTANT: Faye Porter Bonner
PUBLISHING SYSTEMS ADMINISTRATOR: Rick Tucker

Oxmoor House®

For more books to enrich your life, visit
oxmoorhouse.com

contents

Versatile media storage,
page 21

Accessories and organizers,
page 84

Organizing wall,
page 85

foreword

You know the feeling ... you can't find those earrings that exactly match the dress. You've lost that document you know is here somewhere. And how about, "I've lost my keys, and I'm late for the meeting!" Are you sensing the stress? I know I am. With all we have to deal with every day, living amidst clutter only adds to the chaos. I know it firsthand.

Now we can all breathe a sigh of relief, thanks to ORGANIZING MADE EASY from the editors at Southern Living! By following the simple solutions in this bonanza of a book, you can bring a new sense of serenity to everyday life. I've just redone my closet using the ideas on pages 60–65, and I now start my days free of stress. What a welcome change!

This gem of a book is worth its weight in pure gold. With a place for everything and everything in its place, you'll have more control over your life. You'll even have more time for yourself. So go ahead ... give yourself the gift of getting organized. The benefits will astound you! Ahhhh!

Dianne

Dianne Mooney
Senior Vice President & Executive Director
Southern Living At HOME®

getting organized

If you are like most of us, your possessions seem to generate spontaneously until every room in the house is filled with the useless as well as the useful. Keeping the clutter under control requires vigilance and the willpower to actually throw some things away. The following suggestions should help you cut back on clutter.

CLEAR THE CLUTTER

1 IF YOU DON'T NEED IT, DON'T KEEP IT. Unwanted items of all types can be donated to charity or converted into cash at a garage sale. You will benefit either from a tax deduction or actual income, the items will be put to use by other people, and your home will be one step closer to being free of clutter.

2 WEIGH THE COST OF REPLACING AN ITEM AGAINST THE AMOUNT OF SPACE IT TAKES UP. Small, relatively expensive items—such as tools—may be worth keeping even if they are seldom used. Bulky, inexpensive items that you no longer need are definite candidates for disposal.

3 TWO YEARS IS TOO LONG IN THE WORLD OF FASHION. If you haven't worn an outfit in a couple of years, you probably won't ever wear it. Don't hold on to clothes that no longer fit. Most likely, by the time you lose the weight, the clothes will be out of style anyway.

SPLURGE ON STORAGE

Half the job of organizing is having the right tools. Fortunately, there is a wide choice of storage products to help you organize your pared-down possessions. You may even find containers already at hand. Unused suitcases, hatboxes, decorative tins, and wicker baskets can serve to hide clutter, collect like items, and contribute to a room's decor. Getting organized is not a onetime fix, so you'll occasionally need to check on how your storage systems are working.

ORGANIZE EVERYTHING

After your possessions have been pruned, organize your storage needs into four categories: easy access, display, conceal, and long term. Keep things you use or wear at least monthly where they can be easily reached. Display cherished objects by creatively exhibiting them. Keep excess items under wraps by storing them in drawers, cupboards, and closed cabinets.

Relegate belongings used only seasonally or less often, such as ski gear and holiday decorations, to long-term storage on high shelves, in the backs of closets, or in labeled boxes in the attic, basement, or garage.

REMEMBER, CLUTTER CAN NEVER BE ELIMINATED, ONLY CONTROLLED. YOU HAVE TO WORK AT IT TO RESIST THE URGE TO SAVE USELESS ITEMS.

chapter one

entryways

YOUR FRONT ENTRANCE IS A TRANSITION ZONE, an area that allows family and friends to enter and leave your house with maximum pleasure and minimum fuss. Because the entryway offers visitors the first view of your home, its significance is greater than its size. Whether you have a small, cozy entry or a grand, spacious foyer, it should be as efficiently organized as it is warm and welcoming. Stylish furnishings and accessories scaled to fit the front entry space—such as a slim console table, a handy chair, or an attractive mirror—can keep you organized while giving a preview of the decorating style of the rest of your home.

On the following pages you will find dozens of simple ideas for stowing mail, keys, coats, and other items that tend to get deposited at the front entrance. You will also discover great ideas for hidden spaces and how to take advantage of the often-neglected space around the front stairs.

first impressions

Because your entrance hall also functions as your family's traffic route, it's inevitable that purses, jackets, and other day-to-day essentials end up there. Neatly corralling the clutter in a little pocket of space minimizes public view and helps ensure obstacle-free exits and entrances. Fortunately, even a minute front hall has surprising storage capability once you consider all the possibilities.

HOOKS, PEGS, AND OTHER HANG-UPS

Don't overlook the walls of your front hall when floor space is at a premium. Even the smallest entryway has room to add hooks, pegs, and other functional but decorative hang-ups to handle hats, bags, keys, incoming mail, and coats (top and right). Specialty stores, home-improvement centers, and mail-order catalogs present a wealth of practical, good-looking pieces. Or if you're handy, try fashioning your own.

KEY COLLECTORS The tricks to locating keys easily are labeling them, placing them in one spot, and never yielding to the temptation to toss them somewhere else. In the entryway, hang keys from hooks fitted inside a wall-hung cupboard (below).

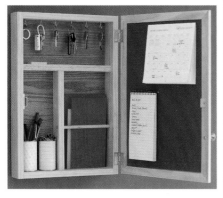

MANAGING MAIL   To simplify the collecting and sorting of mail in your entryway, hang an attractive container on the inside doorknob of your front door. Or add a multitiered organizer to a wall to make it easy to distribute incoming mail to family members and store outgoing mail (below). Place a pretty basket nearby for tossing unwanted items.

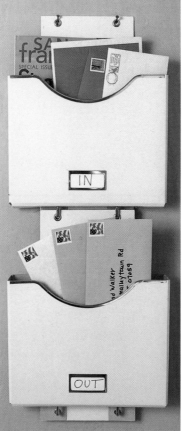

MIRROR IMAGES   The entry is a perfect spot for an attractive mirror outfitted with hooks for purses, hats, keys, and umbrellas (above). A properly equipped mirror will expand storage capacity while reflecting light and visually enlarging the entry area. If space or funds prohibit hanging a large wall-mounted mirror, consider placing a small one on a shelf or hanging a full-length mirror inside the hall-closet door for a quick glance before you leave the house.

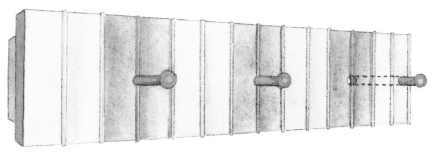

BEADBOARD RACK

Beadboard adds old-fashioned charm to a hang-up. Screw a board of desired length and width into the wall, securing it to studs. Attach a beadboard panel; paint or stain. Insert a row of decorative hooks; or drill holes and insert painted pegs.

shelves and wall units

The size and style of your entrance hall—and your budget—dictate the best types of storage for your possessions. Installing ready-made or ready-to-assemble bracket-mounted and wall-hung shelves is the easiest and least expensive way to provide storage. You can also build your own, with materials and supports from lumberyards or home-improvement centers.

DECORATIVE LEDGES Brightly painted shelves and trimwork create a nice entrance area (below). Hats and rain gear store nicely on a series of hooks. A high ledge makes a handsome display for a series of baskets that can also serve as storage. A stand tucked into the corner keeps umbrellas neatly stored for rainy days.

CUBBIES Cubbyholes are organized, easy-to-reach-into spots where family members can pick up or put away belongings as they dash in or out the front door. Wall-hung (above) or freestanding, cubbies are widely available at retail stores and come in many styles and finishes. When selecting a cubby, be sure its size fits your item-specific needs and the width of the entry. Don't forget about depth, which is particularly important when positioning an organizer near the front door. To lend panache to a cubby, paint the inside a rich color that complements your walls.

MULTIPLE AND GRADUATED SHELVES A series of shelves can store large and small items without overwhelming an entry. Use narrow shelves for collectibles and books (below) and deeper shelves for storage organizers, such as attractive baskets and bins. To unify shelves of differing sizes, use brackets with the same profile. Hooks for frequently used keys can be screwed into side brackets.

BUILT-INS Built-in shelves and wall units are particularly well suited to odd-sized spaces. When recessed into existing walls, they save valuable floor space; when built out from existing walls, they provide floor-to-ceiling storage (above). An amply sized foyer can do double duty as a family library or home office when outfitted with built-ins.

shaker style

"FORM FOLLOWS FUNCTION" describes the Shaker philosophy. The 19th-century religious order is widely celebrated for its practical use of space and design. One of the Shakers' most enduring storage ideas was the high pegboard that lined each room of their dwellings. From hats and coats to brooms and mirrors, everything possible was hung up when it was time to clean. Because beds were too big to lift, wooden casters were added to raise them off the floor.

The Shakers' simple, elegant furniture had no veneers, inlays, or decorative carving. Freestanding cabinets and chests were built without feet or base moldings. Many drawers and closed cupboards were part of a wall, becoming the prototype for today's built-in storage.

functional foyer furniture

Your entry can become much more than a pass-through if you take full advantage of all the space, including acquiring furniture that stores with style. With properly scaled pieces, a front entrance is not only an efficient welcoming zone but also a storage area for virtually anything if your furniture has concealed compartments. If your house lacks a proper entry, try to carve out a few square feet from a room near the front door, perhaps screening it with one or two ornamental yet hardworking pieces of furniture (right).

TABLES AND CHESTS A small console table (left) with a pull-out drawer provides a convenient surface for a key depository and a notepad for messages. Use the often-wasted space underneath the table for stacking vintage suitcases or placing a pair of small ottomans side by side.

Another option is a shallow, slim chest with a series of drawers or shelves. Even a sturdy, low chest can double as a seat and storage piece. Top it with a decorative bowl, and it becomes a one-stop drop for mail.

STAND-INS Fortunately, versatile Victorian space-savers—hat racks, umbrella stands, and hall trees (below)—have regained favor in modern homes. Using minimal floor space, these functional vertical pieces come in a variety of styles and sizes. Be creative in their use: A vintage hat rack, for example, could also hold purses, shopping bags, or lightweight backpacks.

SEATING SPACE Every entry needs a convenient spot close to the front door for people to sit for a moment, lay down a package or purse, and pull off or put on shoes. Some choices are a bench with storage inside (above) or a comfy chair with storage containers below. If you have space, a second chair can be used to hold magazines and books until the chair is needed for extra seating.

DOUBLE-DUTY ACCESSORIES Sturdy baskets, boxes, and trunks with flat lids are other good stand-ins, serving as both furniture and storage units. Use them singly as seats or tables, or pile them up to minimize floor space and maximize their display potential. You can match baskets to the room's decor by painting their exteriors the color of the walls, keeping the interiors natural for best wear. Place baskets or attractive bins in an entry to collect unwanted items for recycling (right) or to separate newspapers, packages, and magazines.

13

chapter two

gathering
places

A GATHERING PLACE IS THE HUB OF A HOUSE, the spot where everyone gets together to chat, play games, watch television, listen to music, or simply relax. It may be a living room, family room, recreation room, live-in dining room, or—in today's open shared-space style—a great room.

Finding places to stow and stash the bits and pieces of daily life in a room where so many activities take place can be a challenge. Concocting a storage strategy that puts the nooks and crannies of your space to work can be as simple as adding storage space where an object is used: a drawer for books in a window seat, slide-out racks for CDs in a media cabinet, wall-mounted shelves for collections.

From custom cabinetry to freestanding furniture, this chapter presents practical ideas and stylish storage solutions for putting everything in its place.

assessing your space

All gathering places are prone to clutter, but different rooms have different storage needs. Organizing a formal living or dining room may focus more on displaying than on hiding things away. Where formal and informal living spaces are combined, however, antiques meet electronics, toys and games jostle photo and art collections, and every square inch of storage must count.

LIVING ROOMS

Like the Victorian parlor from which it descended, the separate living room once served as a home's main gathering place. When a more casual family room was added in the early 1960s, the traditional living room became a special space for greeting guests. With the advent of the open floor plan, it became an oasis for quiet pursuits. Traditional living rooms now are typically used for storing books and audio systems, as well as showcasing artwork or personal possessions.

BOOK NOOK   A bookcase can fit unobtrusively into most living rooms. To increase storage space without detracting from the room's ambience, you might add a bookshelf over the door. A cased opening into the room can be transformed into a mini library with bookshelves built out from the wall (right).

AUDIO CABINET If a living room contains a sound system, one inconspicuous place to house it is behind the doors of a handsome cabinet (below). Upscale retail cabinets in wood and synthetic materials are widely available. Custom-built media cabinets are tailored to fit stereo components.

SMART FURNITURE Installing custom built-ins may be a good way to create unobtrusive storage and display space, but it also helps to buy smart furniture. Look for coffee tables (above) and end tables that have drawers or shelves in addition to pleasing designs. Or substitute a small chest for a side table. For functional storage, don't forget that piano benches and footstools conceal valuable storage space beneath their lift-up seats.

showcasing artwork

YOU NO LONGER HAVE TO HAMMER nails in the wall to hang your fine paintings and prized photos. The latest trend in exhibition is to simply lean artwork against the wall. Pieces are grouped together, often overlapping. Designers believe this creates an informal space, one that lends a bit of irreverence to the pieces.

One way to build your own rotating gallery is to affix a narrow shelf to the wall at the height you would normally hang a picture. Add a front lip or groove to keep frames in place. You can also display artwork on pegs driven into the wall, using the pegs as a base to support the art.

FAMILY ROOMS

A family room hardly needs defining: It's that casual place where everyone "hangs out." It serves so many purposes that creative storage is a must. Look outside the box for ideas. Adjustable shelving, containers on casters, drawers, and television bays (below) competently organize the paraphernalia that tends to clutter family activity spaces. They also artfully display prized collectibles.

STACKABLE MODULES If you can't find modular units to fit your space, think about stackable display cubes. Sold through retail catalogs, container stores, and home-improvement centers, they come in a variety of materials, including galvanized steel (above).

You can make your own from ¾-inch plywood or particleboard cut in the shapes and sizes that suit your space. Nail or screw the boxes together; then sand and finish them with polyurethane or enamel. Add doors to one or more of the boxes to keep the contents hidden. You can make a simple seat by placing two or more boxes together and adding a cushioned top.

TWO-FOR-ONE FURNISHINGS

Storage furniture has obvious advantages: It's movable and can be selected to match your decor and needs. For example, using a metal frame fitted with baskets that slide out like drawers is an inexpensive way to organize writing supplies, magazines, phone books, and games (below). A flat-topped wicker trunk or a chest with drawers becomes a coffee table or an end table. Collect small items, such as coasters, playing cards, and reading glasses, in a basket or pretty bowl placed high enough on a shelf that all you see is the container.

shared spaces

MANY MODERN HOMES COMBINE kitchen, dining, living, and entertaining functions in one big room that has no physical or visual barriers. In this open plan, activity zones and traffic patterns are organized merely by placement of furniture and area rugs.

Storage is paramount in shared spaces, and each space may require a different storage strategy. Functional furniture is invaluable, since it provides storage and delineates activity areas. For example, a console table placed behind a sofa to hold collectibles and other objects also acts as a room divider, setting off the seating area from the kitchen. Low bookcases work as space dividers, too, with a combination of open and closed shelves that allow display room on both sides.

Walls of storage are popular in open spaces. With cabinets, drawers, and shelves, storage walls provide places for items—such as magazines, remote controls, and toys—that accumulate in family living spaces. The walls also offer room to stylishly display decorative items.

ROOM TO PLAY Built-in cabinets and modular systems feature plenty of organized space to stash cards, games, and art supplies. Using baskets, boxes, or trays to hold items for different activities makes it easy to put them away. A roll-around storage bin parks in its own "garage" underneath a cabinet to hide toys (right).

MEDIA ROOMS

Most gathering places revolve around the electronic hearth: the television. But planning a space for watching it is more challenging if the room also serves other purposes. No matter where you put it or how you try to hide it, a media center becomes the focal point of the room.

Major storage and organizing decisions depend on the sizes and shapes of your audio/visual gear. Increasingly complex modern entertainment systems—including televisions, VCRs, DVD players, TiVo recorders, and stereo equipment—require substantial, well-planned storage.

TV VIEWS A television screen should be placed where glare won't interfere with daytime viewing and sight lines are good from anywhere in the room. If a television is concealed in a cabinet or armoire (left), make sure the enclosed space is well ventilated; heat buildup eventually kills transistors and printed circuits. Wide-screen, flat-panel televisions (some as thin as 2 inches) can hang almost anywhere (above). But any television can be removed from the traffic pattern if you put it on a shelf or suspend it from the wall with a special bracket. An attractive container can organize all remotes (below).

ELECTRONIC COMPONENTS

Stack audio and video components in or out of sight, in a custom tower, on a rack, or in furniture adapted for the task. Position components at a height that makes it easy to read their controls (top, facing page).

VIDEOS, DVDs, AND CDs

Versatile storage systems for media accessories come in a variety of combinations that can be amended or extended to fit your changing needs. Hanging CD holders, high-tech cabinets with pull-out shelves or drawers (top, far right), and metal or plastic dividers and trays (bottom, far right) that hold tapes and discs upright are options. Small towers look nice and take up minimal floor space. Choose one without individual, preset slots so that you don't have to shuffle the entire collection to find space for a new piece (right).

standard sizes of media accessories

KNOWING THE SIZES AND SHAPES OF THE MEDIA ACCESSORIES you own ensures that the items fit the allotted spaces. Measure the items you want to organize before building or purchasing a storage unit.

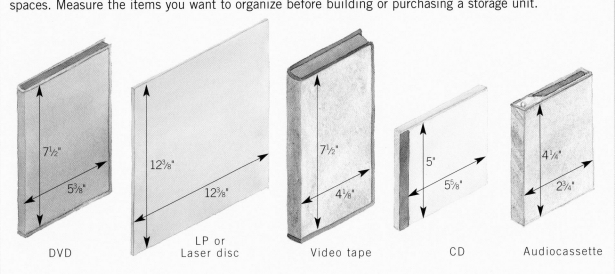

DVD $7\frac{1}{2}$" $5\frac{3}{8}$"

LP or Laser disc $12\frac{3}{8}$" $12\frac{3}{8}$"

Video tape $7\frac{1}{2}$" $4\frac{1}{8}$"

CD 5" $5\frac{5}{8}$"

Audiocassette $4\frac{1}{4}$" $2\frac{3}{4}$"

DINING ROOMS

More than any other room in the house, the dining room has fallen victim to lifestyle changes. Few home owners have space to spare, and what was once a room reserved for family suppers and formal dinners now doubles as a library, sewing studio, or homework headquarters. When the dining area has fuzzy boundaries—such as a breakfast nook or simply a table off the kitchen—efficient space planning and storage help to fully utilize it.

FURNITURE FINDS Mixing good-looking storage pieces with built-in cabinets and shelves creates interest. If pieces are of the same scale, don't worry about using several styles in one room. You can find breakfronts (top, left), sideboards, china cabinets, and buffets (left) in many styles and prices. Any of these dining room pieces make elegant display cases while providing extra shelving.

If you have room for a built-in, a good choice is a wall unit with glass doors and lighted shelves to display china (top, right, facing page). Drawers below hold additional place settings, glasses, and linens.

NOOKS AND CRANNIES A nook can incorporate a freestanding china cabinet. Or an alcove can be filled with a cabinet, shelves, and a wine rack. Even space between the wall studs can be turned into shelves for serving and silver pieces. Or build a shallow cabinet with recycled doors for glassware (right).

A compact cupboard tucked in a corner of the room adds display space. Corner hutches eat up very little floor space, yet a pair can stow almost as much as a breakfront. For a built-in look, buy unfinished versions and paint them to match the trim in your room.

DISH DISPLAY Take advantage of every space to showcase treasures. Install a plate rail on one wall (right), cluster a pottery collection or serving pieces atop a cabinet, or stack china in a compact wrought-iron étagère (left).

space-savers

When you can't stack stereo gear any higher or wedge one more book into your shelves, it's time to think about adding storage space. Every room has unused potential space; you just need to find the spot—and the perfect storage system. The floor-to-ceiling storage walls, versatile shelving, and furniture shown on the following pages are good places to start.

STORAGE WALLS

People are often loath to give up precious floor space for a wall of storage, yet the result is a more functional and beautiful area. Storage walls range from banks of fixed custom shelves (below) to expansive systems with adjustable shelves, open and closed cabinets, and stacks of drawers. Choices include built-in units, modular components, and manufactured cabinets.

BUILT-INS Use built-ins to tie storage seamlessly into your architectural style or to save space in storage-skimpy rooms. They are well suited to odd-sized spaces where storage furniture can't fit: recessed into a wall, under a staircase, around a window, or over a door (right). You can't take built-ins with you when you move, but they will add value to your home.

MANUFACTURED CABINETS   Cabinets like those used in kitchens and bathrooms are another storage option (top, facing page). You can find relatively inexpensive stock models at home-improvement centers and high-end custom creations from a cabinetmaker. As a rule, the semicustom (upgraded stock cabinets available with standard modifications) and custom cabinets are made from higher grade materials and look better, but cost more.

MODULAR SYSTEMS   Versatile and easy to install, modular systems come in a staggering diversity of components and myriad types, styles, and designs. Some lean against or fasten to the wall, eliminating the need for shelf backs or other supports (above). Systems arrive preassembled—you mount components on supports—or ready to assemble. As needs change, manufactured systems can be reconfigured: Shelves can be raised or lowered, drawers refitted, and cabinets moved from one location to another.

SHELF CONTROL

Of all storage components, shelves are the most versatile: They don't take up space as much as create it. And open shelves are more accessible and economical than closed cabinets. Shelves can be fixed or adjustable, pull-out, swivel, or lift-up. They can be installed in cabinets, mounted on walls with brackets or other supports, or added to modular systems. Designers suggest dividing long expanses of shelves into thirds, where space permits, for a more visually pleasing placement. For added interest, vary shelf heights.

WALL-MOUNTED SHELVES Glass, wood, or metal—wall-mounted shelves are good choices for organized living spaces. These shelves showcase possessions and add architectural interest to the space. They fit neatly into empty nooks, hang high above furniture, and display collections, photographs, and art to act as a focal point in the room (above).

MOVABLE SHELVES Adding casters to a shelving unit offers placement flexibility if you regularly change the configuration of furniture. Dress up mobile units with stock molding and decorative trim. For more visual interest, insert fabric-covered foam-core board, cut to fit the height and width of the inside back of the shelving unit (left). It's easy to change the unit's spot—and decorating scheme—according to the season or your evolving taste.

A wealth of shapes, sizes, and styles makes freestanding bookcases easy to situate. These cases increase the storage space in your room without detracting from the decor.

Bookshelves should fit the books you collect. A generous shelf (no deeper than 15 inches) will store most books and electronic gear with ease. Paperbacks need 8- to 10-inch-high shelves. Use upper shelves for standard-size books; put larger volumes, such as art books, on lower shelves (left).

If there's a logical way to return books to a shelf, they are less likely to be left out. Organize books by category, such as novels and nonfiction, the latter grouped by subject. Some people keep libraries intact in one room; others place books where they are read—cookbooks in the kitchen, for example.

standard sizes of books

BOOKS COME IN A VARIETY OF SIZES AND SHAPES, so take an inventory of your library and organize your books by size before you construct or buy a new bookcase.

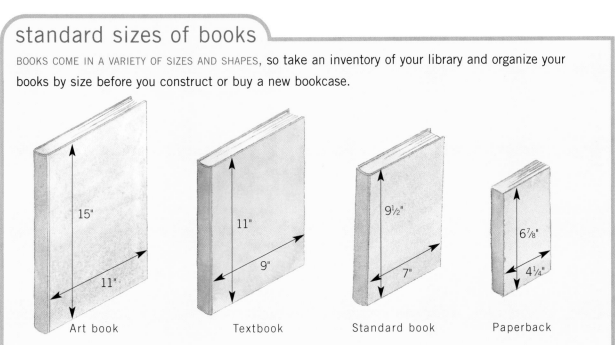

15" / 11"	11" / 9"	9½" / 7"	6⅞" / 4¼"
Art book	Textbook	Standard book	Paperback

best storage furniture

When it's time to purchase furniture, the best storage options will be versatile pieces with added drawers, shelves, or bases for tucking away clutter. Visit flea markets and thrift shops for "secondhand antiques" you can refinish or restore. If your budget doesn't allow for a built-in window seat with pull-out drawers, for example, place a sturdy bench or flat-topped trunk underneath the window, adding a cushion for comfort and baskets or trunks below the bench for added storage. Some workhorses of the storage world are highlighted in the next few pages.

ARMOIRES Having migrated from the bedroom, armoires are now employed as handsome, utilitarian storage spots for gathering places. These popular pieces hold anything from books to bar gear and offer maximum storage in minimal floor space (below). Pick a style that matches your decorating scheme.

APOTHECARY CHESTS Valuable for its many drawers, an apothecary chest is most useful for the organization of small items. When placed prominently in a room, a chest's tidy appearance provides star quality that belies its usefulness (right).

SIDEBOARDS Sideboards and buffets are dining room classics. Ideal for serving food and beverages at mealtime, they also provide space to store silver, linens, serving pieces, wine, and more (below). Also use them as display surfaces for pretty pottery, china, or silver. They can be modified to hold files, sewing supplies, and other useful items.

TRUNKS Flat-topped trunks work well as coffee tables (above), as end tables, or even as extra seating. When outfitted inside with trays and baskets, they organize and contain photos, games, magazines, and newspapers.

29

COFFEE TABLES A coffee table placed in front of a sofa provides convenient space to rest books, magazines, drinks, and snacks; drawers and baskets hide coasters, cards, and games (left). Canvas pockets around a small coffee table offer stand-up places to hold current magazines (below).

OTTOMANS You can convert an ottoman to a coffee table by placing a large wicker tray on top. Choose an ottoman that is an inch or two lower than the sofa and add casters for easy movement. Some ottomans open for extra storage (left).

TANSUS Japanese wooden storage chests and cabinets, called *tansus,* adapt to almost any room. Available in a variety of sizes and shapes, tansus sometimes have interesting stepped shelves. Both antique and reproduction pieces blend effectively with contemporary and traditional designs. If you're buying one to hold a television and sound system, make sure the appliances fit comfortably inside, with enough space for components (right).

CONSOLE AND END TABLES
When equipped with drawers and shelves, console and end tables are invaluable in gathering spaces. The slim profile of the console table enables it to be used almost anywhere storage is needed: behind a couch, in front of a window, or against a wall (left). And end tables do more than just hold lamps: They offer extra surfaces for glasses, books, and special pieces of art (above).

kitchens

ANY KITCHEN—BIG OR SMALL, HIGH STYLE OR NO STYLE—will function efficiently if it's well organized. All you have to do is keep your countertops free of clutter and your kitchen paraphernalia in a logical place where anyone can find it quickly and easily. Sound impossible? Not if you have the right storage solutions for your space.

Whether you're renovating your kitchen or working with what you have, start with good planning. It's definitely easier to reorganize your kitchen during a remodel, but you don't have to invest in new cabinetry to improve your storage capacity. From rattan baskets and shelf maximizers to corner lazy Susans and movable islands, there are many products that can transform your kitchen into a place you don't want to leave.

kitchen primer

Before you begin investigating your options, evaluate your storage needs. Start by opening every drawer and cabinet, and take inventory of your kitchen contents. Are you able to store things near where they are used? Can you find each item without having to move several others aside? And most important, can you get rid of seldom-used kitchenware that takes up valuable space?

SORTING THINGS OUT

Ideally, you want to store items you use regularly in proximity to the kitchen's five main work areas: refrigerator, stove, food preparation, sink/cleanup, and serving. (If your kitchen is large enough, you may have space for an office area as well.) By storing things where you use them, you can cook and clean up quickly and efficiently.

THE WORK TRIANGLE In an efficient kitchen plan, the three most heavily used work areas—the refrigerator, the sink, and the cooktop—should be laid out so that the lines between them form a triangle in which no single leg is shorter than 4 feet or longer than 9 feet. Generally, the counter space within or adjacent to this triangle is used for food preparation. Since this is usually the busiest area of the kitchen, all of your frequently used items—such as utensils, pots and pans, and other culinary equipment—should be stored in the area of first use. Anything that isn't used for preparation or cooking can be stored outside of this work triangle.

Once you know where you want to locate each item, consider how it will be stored. Most items can be sorted into one or more of four functional categories: access easily, display, keep out of sight, or organize. The following pages of this chapter present ideas about how and where to store your kitchen items once you've done the initial work of sorting them into one of these four categories.

typical work triangles

THE MOST EFFICIENT WORK TRIANGLES are found in U-shaped, L-shaped, and galley kitchen designs, as illustrated here. Identify your work triangle, and store the food preparation and cooking items you use regularly inside it.

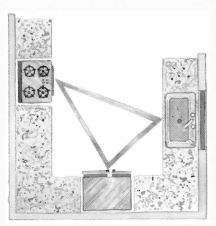

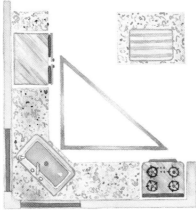

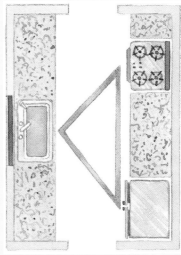

U-SHAPED
When you have enough distance between opposite walls, a U-shaped arrangement provides maximum upper and base cabinet storage, as well as considerable counter space.

L-SHAPED
This work triangle allows for plenty of counter work space. If there is sufficient room for an island in your kitchen, it will increase your overall undercounter storage area.

GALLEY STYLE
This narrow, corridor-style layout makes the best use of a small space. Upper cabinets should cover both walls to maximize your kitchen storage opportunities.

easy access

You daily use some of the items that you store in your kitchen. Others—such as the chafing dish you inherited from your great-aunt Martha—make a brief appearance on special occasions. Once you've sorted out the items you use constantly, you'll want to store them in their proper work areas. When it's easy to find everything, several people can work together without getting in each other's way.

Given the number of ways available to maximize kitchen storage, you shouldn't feel limited by the size or shape of your kitchen. Consider these ideas for rearranging your storage areas so that you can keep everything you use right where you need it.

POTS AND PANS Have them at the ready, nestled in drawers in a base cabinet (below) or hanging from a rack (right). Deep drawers and pull-out shelves are perfect for stockpots. Shallow drawers work well for frying pans and woks.

Store cookie sheets, broiler pans, and cutting boards vertically in a narrow cabinet near the oven (top, facing page). They will be easier to remove and put away than if piled on a shelf. Shallow sliding shelves made of wood or oversize baking pans provide ideal storage for tart pans, cake forms, cookie molds, and other specialty baking items (right).

UTENSILS   Locate spoons, spatulas, whisks, and ladles as close to the stove and food-preparation area as possible. A wide-mouthed ceramic jar (below) or shallow drawers provide ample space for most cooking utensils. When countertop or drawer space is limited, hang utensils from a metal rod or rack mounted to the backsplash or an adjacent wall (below, right).

KNIVES Separate knives and keep them next to the cutting surface. Slots in a cutting board (right), a magnetic wall strip, or a freestanding block (bottom, left) will keep blades safe. When storing knives in a drawer (below), use knife inserts to keep blades from rubbing against each other and becoming dull.

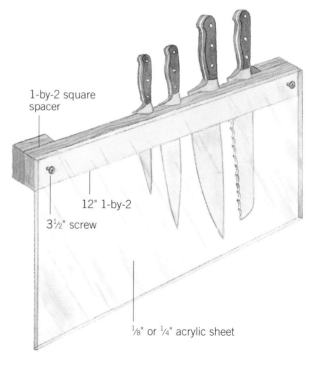

1-by-2 square spacer

12" 1-by-2

3¹⁄₂" screw

¹⁄₈" or ¹⁄₄" acrylic sheet

TRANSPARENT KNIFE RACK

This wall rack can be assembled using 1-by-2 lumber and an ¹⁄₈- or ¹⁄₄-inch sheet of clear acrylic. The acrylic sheet should be at least ¹⁄₂ inch longer than the blade of your longest knife.

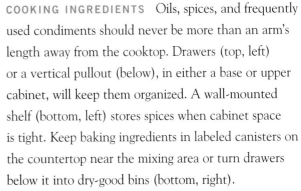

COOKING INGREDIENTS   Oils, spices, and frequently used condiments should never be more than an arm's length away from the cooktop. Drawers (top, left) or a vertical pullout (below), in either a base or upper cabinet, will keep them organized. A wall-mounted shelf (bottom, left) stores spices when cabinet space is tight. Keep baking ingredients in labeled canisters on the countertop near the mixing area or turn drawers below it into dry-good bins (bottom, right).

CLEANING SUPPLIES Use the space under your sink to store cleaning materials and garbage if you don't have room for a designated pull-out bin within your base cabinetry. There are many configurations of pull-out baskets (above), towel racks, and bins designed specifically for this space, as well as those that attach to the inside of a cabinet door. A sink-front tilt-out drawer (above) provides a resting place for vagabond sponges and scrub brushes. Consider hanging your dish drainer and paper towels from a metal-rod wall system next to the sink instead of having them take up valuable counter or undercounter space.

wheelchair access

ACCESSIBILITY IS NOT just a convenience but a necessity if you are in a wheelchair. When planning your kitchen, everything you use regularly should be comfortably within your seated reach.

Ideally, the space below the sink and cooktop should be left open to accommodate your wheelchair. The dishwasher can be elevated so you don't have to bend over when you insert and remove dishes. The microwave should be placed no higher than the countertop.

Most items should be stored 15 to 48 inches from the floor—on the countertop or in pull-out vertical pantries, shelves, and drawers. You can outfit the backsplash behind a wheelchair-accessible countertop with a metal rod and then hang utensils, pots, and pans from it. While most overhead storage is off-limits to anyone in a wheelchair, pull-down shelves available from specialty manufacturers can be mounted in upper cabinets, enabling you to take advantage of once-unreachable storage.

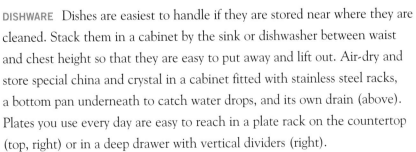

DISHWARE Dishes are easiest to handle if they are stored near where they are cleaned. Stack them in a cabinet by the sink or dishwasher between waist and chest height so that they are easy to put away and lift out. Air-dry and store special china and crystal in a cabinet fitted with stainless steel racks, a bottom pan underneath to catch water drops, and its own drain (above). Plates you use every day are easy to reach in a plate rack on the countertop (top, right) or in a deep drawer with vertical dividers (right).

on display

As the kitchen has become a central meeting place for family and friends, presentation has become a priority for many home owners. It is now fashionable to display almost everything in the kitchen—from dishes and pots to gourmet oils and vinegars. Cabinetmakers and storage manufacturers have risen to the occasion with attractive display cases, baskets, canisters, and racks.

THE PROS AND CONS

The most obvious benefit of keeping your wares out in the open is that they are easy to reach. And a tasteful display can add character to your kitchen. But before you unhinge your cabinet doors and install open shelving, consider what you have to display and what kind of housekeeper you are. You should be prepared to keep these displays in perfect order—if items are thrown randomly onto shelves and into baskets, your kitchen will have a sense of chaos.

Additionally, displayed items require frequent cleaning. Kitchen paraphernalia on open shelves or in baskets collects dust. Unless you regularly use and wash items, such as your everyday dishes and glassware, you may want to keep them behind closed doors.

OPEN SHELVING   The most straightforward way to show off your collections is with open shelving. Shelves can be built inside a cabinet box, float on the wall (right), or be suspended by cables. They can be white, stained wood, or brightly colored to complement

what they are holding (above); or they can be made from wire or galvanized metal. Open shelves can be placed above or under the counter, and you can even string them across a fixed window as a place to hold fresh herbs. You can also buy stand-alone units of open shelving in wood or metal.

GLASS DOORS Use cabinets with glass doors on one or both sides (top, right) to display items you want seen but protected from dust and grease. If you like the sense of openness glass cabinets provide but not the work required to keep their contents in order, you can choose from a wide range of translucent glasses that obscure what's on the other side (right).

ON THE RACK Consider racks that hang on the wall or under wall cabinets for holding and displaying a collection of mugs and teacups (below), gourmet oils and vinegars, and even stemware (bottom). Or you can hang a rack from the ceiling to display a favorite set of pots and pans (right).

BASKETS Constructed from rattan or wire, baskets are used to show off produce and sundries in more informal kitchens (above). They can rest on open shelves above or below the countertop (right). To display a collection of baskets, hang them decoratively from the ceiling.

art of arrangement

WHETHER YOU HAVE a special collection you want to showcase or open shelves to fill, you can create an attractive display by following a simple rule: Group items together that share a common characteristic, such as type or color (or a combination of the two).

Any group of objects will look agreeable together if they have a similar or complementary shape or color. The simplest displays gather identical items, such as a line of plates or bowls. A display becomes more complex when you group a set of dishware of identical or complementary colors on the same shelf.

If you have a collection of similar items with different shapes, such as teapots or vases, arrange them according to height or width. Condiments in bottles and spices in jars make nice displays if grouped so that their shapes and labels complement each other.

Once you have arranged basic groupings, enhance them by throwing in a visual surprise. A glass pitcher can add interest to a display of colored dishes. Silver mugs complement a group of heavy ceramic bowls.

In the end, your eye is the best judge of what is most appealing. Expect to move things around before you find the arrangement that best represents your style and adds the most character to your kitchen.

hidden assets

The greatest advances in kitchen storage have been made in the storage systems that fit inside or under cabinets. You can purchase them with new cabinetry or as items you install yourself. Look for these inserts at kitchen and bath dealers, at home-improvement stores and storage-oriented retailers, and over the Internet.

THE PROFICIENT PANTRY Use the pantry for storing non-perishable foods and dry goods. You can create a pantry from a dedicated cabinet, a walk-in closet, or freestanding shelving units. The key to a successful pantry is having every item in view. Anything at the back of a deep stationary shelf—especially one high up or near the floor—risks being overlooked.

If a standard upper, base, or tall cabinet serves as a pantry, you can retrofit it with a vertical pull-out system in wood, plastic, or wire (above). Manufacturers make fold-out inserts for pantries in wood, plastic, or stainless steel. If you use a fold-out insert, you may have enough space to hang small racks on the inside of the door (top, right). Wrapping shallow shelves around the interior of a small pantry closet will keep your stored foods and dry goods in view (right).

Replacing stationary shelves with wire baskets or shallow drawers on durable, full-extension drawer slides (above) keeps pantry items categorized and easy to reach when pulled out.

APPLIANCE STORAGE   Finding the right place for an appliance is often a dilemma because most large appliances, such as food processors and bread machines, are cumbersome. An appliance garage with wooden or glass doors hides appliances at the back of the counter (below, left and right). Or you can install a lift-up shelf in a base cabinet to hold a large mixer or processor. Inserting a power head for a blender into a countertop or drawer leaves you with only the container and blades to store. Undercounter or wall mounts for coffeemakers and toasters are also available.

PRODUCE PRESENTATION Replacing a solid drawer with wire, rattan, or perforated plastic baskets on drawer slides provides a handy, off-the-counter spot for potatoes, onions, or fruits (below and right). Or remove a base cabinet door and store produce in baskets on the open shelves.

BREAD DRAWERS Rattan baskets turned into pull-out drawers make a great place to stach wrapped bread (right). You can also turn any drawer that's up to 24 inches wide into a bread box with wood, clear plastic, metal, or terra-cotta inserts. Many inserts come with a hinged or sliding top to keep the bread fresh. Some even come with a wooden top so that you can cut the bread right where you store it.

HIDING THE TRASH For years the only place to hide the kitchen wastebasket was under the sink. Now, trash includes recycling and is divided into categories, necessitating more than one bin (right). There are many base-cabinet trash inserts that pull out and include room for two or three bins. Some come with built-in wire bins, while others have openings for plastic garbage cans. These undercounter pullouts can also store dog and cat food (below).

UNEXPECTED SPACES

Sometimes, finding room in your kitchen takes ingenuity as well as good organization. You may need to look beyond the traditional storage options to increase your kitchen's capacity. If so, it's time to take advantage of hidden air space you don't normally use.

UNDER THE UPPER Manufacturers make storage units that mount under the upper cabinets and are completely hidden when not in use. The most common are cookbook holders, knife blocks, and spice racks. If you don't have room on your countertop for a radio or CD player, choose one specially made for this often-wasted space (right).

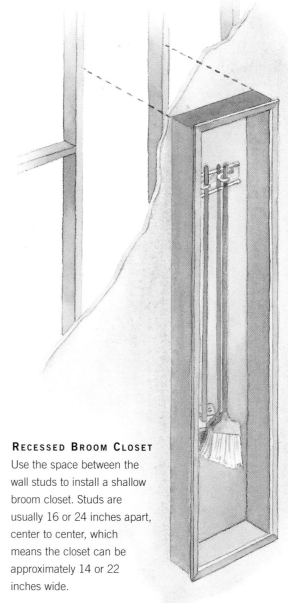

BEHIND THE TOE KICK Most kitchen base cabinets are raised 4 or 5 inches off the floor. Generally a baseboard, or "toe kick," runs the length of the cabinetry to keep dust from collecting below it. If you cut a section of baseboard, you can fill the space with shallow drawers that hide anything from serving dishes to silver flatware pieces to lightbulbs (above). Or you can use this space to store a folding stepladder.

RECESSED BROOM CLOSET
Use the space between the wall studs to install a shallow broom closet. Studs are usually 16 or 24 inches apart, center to center, which means the closet can be approximately 14 or 22 inches wide.

IN THE WALL In most frame construction there is a space behind the wallboard and between the studs that is about 4 inches deep. It's not big enough for a full cabinet, but it is the perfect depth for spice shelves (left), dish displays, or an ironing-board cabinet. If you have a narrow bit of wall space, this might be a good place to build a shallow cabinet for your broom and dustpan. New products are continually being introduced that use this wall space, including toaster and paper-towel cabinets.

freestanding furniture

IF YOU STILL DON'T HAVE enough room after maximizing the cabinetry in your kitchen, consider using a piece of furniture. Movable islands (top, right), cabinets, and tables, which come in many styles and sizes, can provide extra work surfaces or additional drawers and shelves. Special features include marble butcher-block tops, bottle shelves, and dish-towel racks. Move furniture with casters out of the way when not in use.

Another attractive idea is to fit an antique armoire with vertical and horizontal shelves to provide more dish and food storage or to house a cookbook collection. Transform an old bedroom bureau or library cabinet into a kitchen storage and serving area. Shallow drawers are perfect for linen storage (above, left), while deep drawers work well for big serving bowls and china.

For a contemporary look, add a metal baker's rack (bottom, right) or modular wood shelving for more storage. Easy to assemble and relatively inexpensive, these units can stand up against a wall or be used as room dividers.

organizing the clutter

Many kitchens have at least one cabinet or drawer that is a catchall for the equipment that doesn't have an obvious storage spot. The garlic press, eggbeater, and rolling pin compete for space in the drawer. Dry goods and canned foods are difficult to find when randomly placed on shelves. Messages and coupons left loose on the countertop are often overlooked or lost. It doesn't have to be that way.

CABINET APPOINTMENTS

With a little ingenuity and the right retail purchases, you can organize your dishware, dry goods, and gadgets inexpensively with ready-made products and create more space within your cabinets. Shelf maximizers, risers, and special holders increase the storage capacity of a simple shelf while bringing order to it.

PLATE RACKS Use a plate rack to keep plates from chipping or rubbing against each other. These racks provide vertical slots for plates (right).

SHELF MAXIMIZERS To double or even triple your usable space and protect your dishware at the same time, use a maximizer to store more than one layer of items on a shelf. Stack cups and saucers above dinner plates and bowls above platters on the same shelf (right). Maximizers come in different shapes, styles, and materials, such as wire, wood, and acrylic. Some sit on shelves and some hang below, providing shallow spaces for flat serving dishes or linens.

CABINET PULLOUTS Transform an inefficient cabinet quickly and inexpensively with pull-out wire drawers (top, facing page), plastic baskets, or vertical dividers you can buy at home-improvement or home-storage centers. While the cabinet may take some time to clean out initially, these storage solutions can be installed easily and will save you time in the future.

TIERED RACKS Risers and tiered racks won't expand your shelf space but will enable you to see everything stored on the shelf. Use them for canned goods, spices, and condiments (top, right).

SPECIALTY HOLDERS If you don't have a drawer perfectly proportioned to hold foils and plastic wraps, hang them on the wall or on the back of a door in a holder made for that purpose (below). Store plastic and paper bags in door-mounted holders just inside your sink cabinet.

LID HOLDERS To organize lids that don't fit anywhere else, use a lid holder. Some styles, such as door and shelf racks (right), hold pot lids vertically so that they won't get lost among your pots and pans. Lid holders also come on pull-out tracks that mount to a shelf (below, right). A large plastic mixing bowl or square container will conveniently hold lids for plastic containers of different sizes.

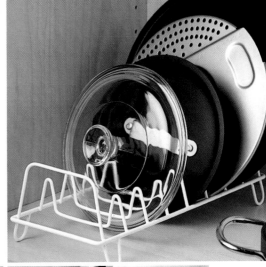

wine accommodations

MANY PEOPLE KEEP SEVERAL BOTTLES of wine in the kitchen for either drinking or cooking. Wine is often stored standing among other bottles and cans in a cabinet or left cluttering the countertop. But the best way to store wine is on its side, away from direct sunlight and any direct heat sources, such as the stove, oven, or dishwasher. If you have young children, be sure to store it out of their reach.

Retail stores offer a variety of racks and bottle holders that fit inside a cabinet or mount under a wall cabinet. If you're buying new cabinetry, you can include square, diamond-shaped, or circular openings for wine bottles. When cabinet space is limited, build a freestanding wine box that stores wine safely on its side.

Whatever you use to hold wine in the kitchen, keep in mind that wine needs a stable environment to maintain its flavor. Since temperatures can fluctuate dramatically in the kitchen, store wine there for only a short period.

WINE CUBE

You can store a dozen bottles of wine in this wooden box on your countertop or floor. The cube is made of four 12-inch-square sheets of softwood, such as pine or poplar, and one back sheet cut to fit. Two notched sheets of plywood fit together inside the cube to create four sections of storage.

DYNAMIC DRAWERS

With the right kinds of organizers, you can eliminate chaos in your drawers. To maximize their capacity, you should match the size of the drawer to the items you want to store. For instance, store flatware, utensils, and linens in a shallow drawer—14 to 18 inches wide for flatware and utensils, and up to 30 inches wide for linens. Pots, pans, and dishes fit best in 12-inch-deep drawers. Once you determine what will go in each drawer, select organizers that fit the drawers and contain the items in them.

UTENSIL AND FLATWARE TRAYS

These helpers separate each type of item into its appropriate compartment. Utensil trays have four or more wide compartments for serving pieces and cooking utensils. You can create your own compartments in a drawer using wood, cardboard, or plastic slats that run vertically or horizontally across the drawer's surface (above).

Most flatware trays come with compartments for knives, salad forks, dinner forks, teaspoons, and soup spoons. There are also trays that stack so that a shorter tray slides above a full-size one in a single drawer (left).

DISH AND BOWL ORGANIZERS
Different styles of organizers enable you to store plates and serving pieces inside deep drawers. A vertical-rack system protects plates from chipping. A Peg-Board system with removable dividers keeps stacked dishes, mixing bowls, and serving pieces in place so that they don't slide around and knock into each other in the drawer (right).

DRY AND BAKING GOODS Dry goods, such as beans and nuts, store well and are easy to locate in glass-fronted drawers lined with sheet metal. Outfitting a top drawer with plastic bins keeps flour, sugar, salt, and other baking ingredients at your fingertips (above).

LINENS Relegate everyday linens—such as place mats, tablecloths, and napkins—to wide, shallow drawers close to the serving and eating areas. Use cardboard dividers cut to fit the length and width of your drawers to organize place mats, napkins, and napkin rings into compartments (above).

THE COMMAND CENTER

The kitchen is the one room you can be fairly certain that all family members will pass through during the course of the day. It is the obvious place for posting the week's calendar—if you happen to be so organized—and leaving messages. But small pieces of paper, coupons, and messages are easily misplaced when they don't have an assigned place. A message center not only organizes paperwork in the kitchen but also keeps your family in touch.

WALL SYSTEMS The easiest way to leave messages is on a blackboard or tackboard (right). These are easy to make; but if you are not so inclined, many retailers sell framed boards that do double duty as either chalkboards or felt pen-and-magnetic boards. Some boards

are configured as shallow boxes, with slots on the sides to hold letters; others have hooks below for hanging keys.

If you have an expanse of unused wall space, you can cut a hole in the wallboard and build a narrow cabinet with cubbies, drawers, and tackboard into the recessed area between the wall studs (right).

INSIDE A DOOR When you don't have any wall space to spare, a wall cabinet or pantry door provides a vertical surface for a message board. Line the inside or outside of the door with tackboard, Peg-Board, or blackboard material; keep a box of notepaper, pencils, and tacks or chalk on a shelf inside the cabinet. With a little extra craftsmanship, an end cabinet can be fitted with tackboard that is hidden behind a door (left).

chapter four

beds & baths

BEDROOMS AND BATHROOMS can be welcoming retreats if organized properly. The best way to ensure a relaxing atmosphere is to have a dedicated spot for everything, from clothes to personal items.

A bedroom is a wonderful refuge from the hustle and bustle of daily life. A large bedroom provides many storage options, especially if you have a walk-in closet. A small bedroom requires more inventive storage strategies. Regardless of the size of the room, you may be surprised at how many ways you can bring order to it.

The bathroom has undergone a great transformation over time. No longer simply utilitarian, today's space tends to be large, compartmentalized, and carefully detailed. The search for additional storage has created ingenious, attractive solutions for space-shy baths. From powder rooms to master baths, you'll find fresh ideas you can use for any bathroom.

master bedrooms

The master bedroom, unlike other bedrooms in the house, is designed for adults who work hard all day and want to rest in the evening. While some bedrooms double as offices, the master bedroom is more often used for reading, changing clothes, and sleeping. So you should store only items related to these activities there, with the exception of art or artifacts you include to give the room its own personality.

CLOSETS THAT WORK

Ideally, you want some kind of useful system that enables you to hide the majority of your clothing behind closed doors. Almost every master bedroom has some kind of closet where you can store your clothes, shoes, and accessories. Many older closets—whether they are cavernous walk-ins or narrow reach-ins with single hanging rods—have wasted or unusable space. With the proper management, you can make either more efficient by installing a custom-built, do-it-yourself, or prefabricated closet system.

Limit the number of hanging rods to the amount of clothing you need to hang and then add as many drawers and shelves as you can fit in the remaining space. Having drawers, shelves, and clothes rods all in one place helps keep clothing and accessories organized (left).

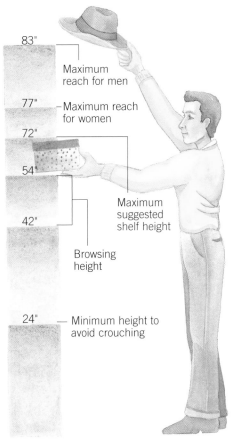

83"	Maximum reach for men
77"	Maximum reach for women
72"	
54"	Maximum suggested shelf height
42"	Browsing height
24"	Minimum height to avoid crouching

IDEAL SHELF HEIGHT FOR ADULT REACH

Place regularly used items between waist height and eye level. Use lower and upper shelves for less frequently used objects. Heights are based on a 5-foot 7-inch man and a 5-foot 4-inch woman.

RANGE OF MATERIALS Depending on your budget and taste, create a closet system from wood, MDF (medium-density fiberboard), wire racks, or hanging bags. It is easy to put something together yourself, using a combination of units—such as wire-basket drawers for folded clothing, hanging rods for shirts and pants, shelves for purses and shoes, and assorted storage containers (above)—purchased at a home-improvement store.

HEIGHT CONSIDERATIONS Anything you use all the time should be within your normal reach. Use the highest and lowest shelves or drawers only for items you keep stored away for unusual weather or special events. The maximum reach for the average woman is 77 inches; for a man, it is 83 inches. You'll have to crouch down to reach anything located under 2 feet high.

SHELVES Great storage for shirts, sweaters, and handbags, shelves come in various depths to accommodate different items. They can be placed above both upper and lower hanging bars if you plan the space properly. To make a standing unit, run shelves between lengths of bars or install them at one end of the closet, using the wall for support (left). Pull-out shelves work well for keeping stacks of folded items in order.

DRAWERS A tower of drawers or wire baskets provides a way to organize your folded clothes within the closet (above). Many prefabricated units allow you to combine drawers or wire baskets and shelves in a single tower.

freestanding wardrobes

IF YOUR BUDGET and closet space are limited, purchase space-saving mobile wardrobes in all wood, wood and glass, metal, or canvas over a metal frame. If you don't wish to keep a wardrobe in the open, you can hide it behind a curtain or tapestry and wheel it out when needed. Wardrobes come in different widths, with or without shelves and drawers.

Another option is to make a rotating Swedish storage tower, with shelves on one side for folded clothes and a full-length mirror on the other (right). For the able do-it-yourselfer, it is an easy project made of a three-sided rectangular box set on a rotating pedestal. The box can be framed with wooden molding to give it more style. Use a hardwood that matches other furniture in your room, stencil designs on its sides, or paint each surface a different bright color.

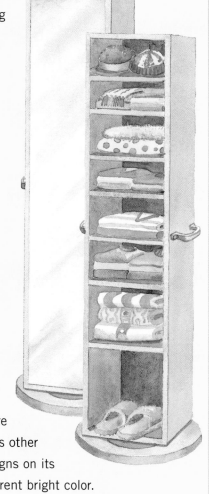

HANGING RODS To maximize storage space, combine single and double rods within the closet (left). Generally, short garments—such as blouses, short skirts, pants, and jackets—need 36 to 42 inches of hanging space. Long items—such as dresses, long skirts, and winter coats—require 66 to 69 inches.

Before determining how long your hanging rods should be, take an inventory of your clothing. How much total width do you need for short garments? How wide a space do you need for long items? Now is a good time to decide whether you need all the clothes that are hanging in your closet. If you haven't worn something in two years, consider giving it away.

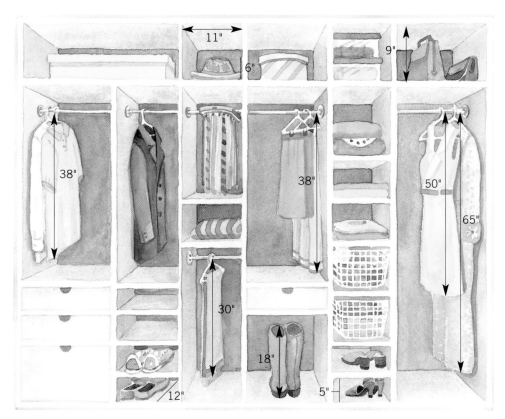

STANDARD CLOSET MEASUREMENTS
This illustration provides measurements that are based on average adult heights and styles of clothes. Check your clothing against these measurements. The height of any hanging space should be about 4 inches larger than your longest piece of clothing.

ORGANIZING YOUR CLOSETS AND DRAWERS

Having a good closet system in place is half the battle in organizing your bedroom. But how many times have you arranged your hanging clothes and refolded pants, shirts, and sweaters only to find everything in confusion by the end of the week? There's no reason to have messy drawers, shelves, or closets with all the different organizing accessories on the market today. Give yourself a little help with some of the following ideas.

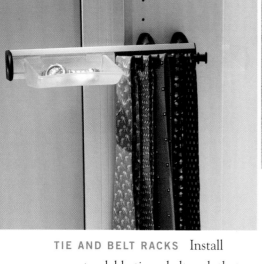

TIE AND BELT RACKS Install an extendable tie or belt rack that slides out for easy access to the back or side of your closet. You can even attach a tray that holds watches and small accessories (above). Wooden hangers with pegs, wall-mounted racks, and rows of hooks are also simple solutions. Or manage a vast tie collection with a motorized tie rack; these plug into any standard wall outlet using an AC adapter or can be operated using batteries.

DRAWER DIVIDERS To create order out of the mass of clothing and accessories in your drawers, use dividers. Multicompartment plastic or cardboard dividers come in different configurations: various sizes and shapes for lingerie and small squares for socks, stockings, and belts (below). Use clear plastic rectangular boxes to organize briefs, lingerie, or T-shirts. Cedar drawer boxes keep moths away from wool sweaters, socks, and scarves.

BOXES Open or lidded, boxes are widely available in different sizes to store shoes, sweaters, shirts, and blankets—or just about anything else you keep in your bedroom. These boxes are made of wood, rattan, plastic, and canvas. Lacquered pasteboard boxes with lids will add a little color to your closet storage while also protecting your items from dust (left). Clear boxes make it easy to identify contents quickly, but you can also buy opaque boxes with label holders. Use large open boxes situated on the floor to keep shoes in one place.

JEWELRY ORGANIZERS The obvious place to store jewelry is in a jewelry box on a bureau in your bedroom. If you don't have enough surface space for a large box, hang your earrings from a cheese grater (below) or stack your rings on an upside-down metal funnel. A shallow drawer is another convenient spot for tucking jewelry out of the way (bottom). Check out retail stores for inserts that fit most drawers or try a kitchen-drawer organizer divided into compartments.

Another option is to roll up necklaces or bracelets in padded flatware bags and tuck them among your lingerie. Or purchase a jewelry bag with multiple pockets and hang it between clothes in the closet.

SHOE RACKS Adding a shoe rack to your closet will not only keep your shoes together in pairs but also will make them easier to find. You can set a shoe rack or cubby system on the floor under your hanging clothes (above). However, consider storing your shoes off the floor at waist height for better visibility and easier access.

If you don't have many pairs of shoes, you can line them up on a shelf between two rods of short hanging garments. Clear plastic boxes stacked on a shelf keep shoes visible and accessible (right). Soft plastic or canvas shoe bags that hang from your closet rod or the inside of a door free up floor and wall space.

Many shoe-storage systems are made to be added on to, either vertically or horizontally, as your shoe collection grows.

DUAL-FUNCTION FURNITURE

If you have done everything possible to increase your closet's storage capacity and still have more to put away, you don't have to resort to using the hall closet. From headboards that stow books and photos to nightstands that stash bedtime essentials, clever bedroom furniture should serve more than one purpose if you are short on storage space.

CABINETS Antique or modern cabinets, such as armoires, add character to the room and give you more space to hide your clothes, blankets, and other personal items (below and right). They can be customized to store a television or stereo or to double as a desk unit.

BUREAUS, DRESSERS, AND NIGHTSTANDS Bureaus. dressers, and chests are versatile storage pieces that organize and conceal clothes and accessories. They come in just about every style and material imaginable—choose an item that complements your decorating style and fulfills your storage needs.

Almost every master bedroom has some kind of nightstand for an alarm clock, lamp, and water glass. Ideally, the nightstand includes a drawer for those items you don't want to keep on display, such as night cream, glasses, and maybe a remote control (bottom, left, facing page). If your bedside table has shelves, use stylish containers to camouflage nightstand necessities. If bookshelves flank your bed, convert one shelf at mattress height into a pull-out table and use it as your bedside table at night.

STORAGE IN A SEAT A bench or ottoman purchased or made with a hinged top that opens to reveal a storage cavity gives you more space for stowing bedroom items. A simple open bench with vertical dividers and a cushioned top functions both as a place to sit and as a stash for purses, shoes, and bedtime reading materials (left). A steamer trunk or stack of old leather suitcases placed at the foot of the bed provides great storage for folded items, such as blankets or winter woolens.

BEHIND AND UNDER THE BED Headboards and frames don't have to be simple vertical planes. Many wonderful headboards incorporate both bookshelves and cubbies without taking up much extra room. And don't forget the space under the bed. Frames outfitted with drawers (above) and shallow rolling bins that tuck under the bed provide a wide storage area for large items, such as blankets and extra pillows, that might not fit easily into your closet or bureau. Keep them in breathable bags or boxes to protect against dust.

kids' bedrooms

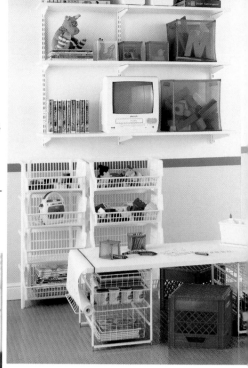

For a child, unorganized space can turn a cornucopia of toys into a nightmare of objects. What parent hasn't heard the words "I have nothing to do"? They come from a child who can't make sense of all the clutter. Most children love to sort from an early age and will keep their rooms clean if they have places to put everything. The key to storage in a kid's room is to start with an expandable system that will work for the child as he or she grows.

AT KIDS' HEIGHT

Children play, entertain, study, and sleep in their bedrooms. They can't do any of these things well if their floors are littered with clothes and toys and if their desks and beds are in a constant state of disarray. Storage is the obvious solution to chaos, but it is efficient only if it places things within reach. Designing storage for kids is unique in that everything has to be stored to their scale.

SHELVES Low shelving is critical in any child's room. The maximum shelf height for a 3-foot 9-inch child should be 45 inches. A 5-foot 2-inch teenager can reach up to 66 inches. Floating bookshelves provide some flexibility (left), as they can be installed at low heights when the child is young and moved as he or she grows. If you use a decorative stand-alone bookcase, place only display items on upper shelves.

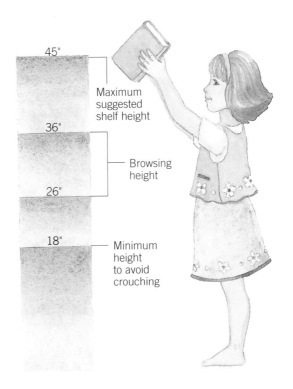

45"
Maximum
suggested
shelf height

36"
Browsing
height

26"

18"
Minimum
height
to avoid
crouching

IDEAL SHELF HEIGHT FOR KIDS' STORAGE
Store toys and books on bottom shelves so that they are easily accessible when children are playing on the floor. Place display items on the upper shelves. Heights are based on a 3-foot 9-inch child.

One of the easiest ways to create an expandable shelf system is to use stackable storage cubes fastened together (above). As the child grows, you can easily add height to the tower.

HANDY HANG-UPS A pegboard that lines the wall or shelves with hooks (right) can hold jackets, backpacks, belts, and hats. Either can also hold laundry bags or hanging bags with compartments that are ideal for storing stuffed animals, small toys, and even shoes. Run a line of pegboard at a common chair height (about 36 inches from the floor) within your child's reach or place a row of decorative hooks at your child's current height and raise them each year.

Since most young kids have few hanging clothes, one or two short rods set low to the ground are sufficient in the early years. Outfit the rest of the closet with drawers and shelves, altering the ratio of rods to drawers and shelves as needed (left).

ROLLING CARTS If your child has an ample closet, use rolling carts with drawers to store toys or supplies out of sight (below). Mobile furniture allows a child to control his or her environment to a point and to move toys around to suit immediate needs for floor space. A rolling cart with a solid top converts into a table for assembling puzzles or playing games.

A PLACE FOR EVERYTHING

While it is helpful for kids to be able to see their belongings in order to find them quickly, not everything needs to be stored out in the open. A hook or two will hang tomorrow's outfit, but the remainder of a child's clothing can be tucked away in a bureau or closet. Sporting equipment, art supplies, and games can be organized in closets, cabinets, or desks.

THE CLOSET A child's closet can be configured in much the same way as an adult's, with hanging space, shelves, and drawers. But since clothes will change in size as the child grows, choose a closet system that can be easily modified over time (right).

DESKS By the time a child starts school, he or she will need a desk for doing homework and keeping school supplies. The desk should have a shelf for notebooks and a drawer for pencils and paper. Since children of all ages use computers, find a desktop large enough to hold one (above). Many new models of desks come equipped with keyboard trays and CPU holders.

ARMOIRES Armoires that are designed for children's rooms can house a hanging rod, shelves, and drawers for clothes and linens. Use baskets with colorful liners on shelves to round up toys, books, and games (above). Some armoires come with built-in desks. The inside of a door can be lined with a blackboard or tackboard on which kids can draw or hang art.

TOY CHESTS AND BINS Toy chests are great for storing large items, such as blocks, balls, and bats; they can also serve as a bench. But avoid keeping small items in a toy chest, as they will get mixed up with everything else and be difficult to find. A frame outfitted with sliding plastic bins of varying sizes accommodates both small and large toys (right).

KEEPING IT IN ORDER

Once you have the main furniture in place, it's time to organize all the toys and books on shelves or in drawers or boxes. To do this effectively, break down all your children's toys into the smallest categories possible. For instance, separate miniature stuffed animals from their larger cousins or divide up toy cars and trucks. When you figure out how many categories of toys your child has accumulated, you will know how many boxes, baskets, or drawer dividers to buy.

TOY TOTES Another simple toy-containment solution is a large tote bag (above). You can use it to hold your child's favorite playthings and easily transport it from room to room. Totes are the right height for helping kids to start cleaning up their own toys.

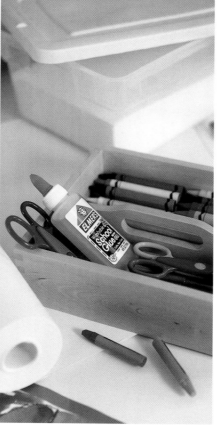

BOXES, BASKETS, AND BINS
Clear or colored boxes or baskets with cotton liners can be stacked on the floor or on shelves and then filled with sporting equipment or toys that have been sorted into various categories. Label them with a word or drawing so that young children know where to return items after playing with them. Compact boxes are perfect for small blocks, cars, and doll clothes and accessories (above).

DRAWER INSERTS Ordinarily used in the kitchen, drawer inserts can be placed in plastic boxes with lids to organize art supplies. Keep crayons and markers in one box and paper supplies in another (left).

UNDERBED STORAGE If your child does not have a loft, trundle, or captain's bed, it's still possible to take advantage of the empty space underneath. A variety of underbed containers are available at retail stores and through catalogs (right). Before you buy, measure the space below the child's bed to make sure the container will fit.

A flat wooden platform on casters not only lets you store things under the bed but also can be used as a roll-away hard play surface. Paint the surface with blackboard paint so that a child can use it to draw (below).

HANGING POCKETS Custom wall hangings with pockets (right) and hanging shoe bags offer clever storage off the floor. Attach them to the wall or the back of a door and then use them to store small items, from stuffed animals to miniature car collections.

grand bathrooms

No matter how big the bathroom, storing the myriad supplies is always a challenge. Basically, there are only three ways to store belongings in a bathroom: hang them on the walls, add freestanding furniture, and build in cabinets and shelves. An effective strategy usually combines all three approaches, but the logical place to start when planning better bathroom storage is with cabinetry.

CAPABLE CABINETS

Oversize vanities, floor-mounted and wall-mounted cabinets, and recessed (between the wall studs) units are the workhorses of bathroom storage. These cabinets help you keep decorative objects on view while hiding mundane items behind doors. Shallow cabinets take up less floor space and offer greater accessibility; deeper cabinets are best reserved for towels and larger supplies.

VANITY FAIR The most useful vanities come with a variety of drawers and shelves. Vertical pull-out shelves fitted with towel bars keep hand towels at the ready on either side of a sink (above). Stow bulky objects and supplies around plumbing fixtures under the sink. To maximize efficiency in areas with limited space, add a tilt-out drawer to serve as a clothes hamper.

VINTAGE VANITIES Though you will lose some space to the sink and plumbing fixtures, turning a vintage piece into a vanity adds character to a bath. A fully plumbed antique cabinet hides storage behind handsome doors (above); furniture with drawers can be customized to wrap around a sink trap. Waxing the wood is one way to protect the finish of a vintage piece; for other suggestions, see "Wood and Water" on page 83.

If you like the antique look but prefer to use materials fashioned specially for a bath, you can find new furniture-quality vanities with fitted sinks and stone counters made to look like traditional commodes. Available at bath and kitchen stores as well as home centers, these attractive pieces combine old-fashioned style with today's sensible storage options.

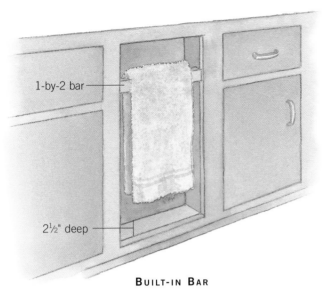

1-by-2 bar

2½" deep

BUILT-IN BAR

If your vanity lacks a towel bar, it's easy to add one just below and slightly to the side of the sink. A 1-by-2 bar allows you to grab a towel without having to search for it. Make the pocket 2½ inches deep and finish its surfaces to match the cabinet facing. The bar itself is inset ½ inch from the cabinet front.

SIDE CABINETS Designers use pedestal, vessel, and wall-mounted sinks, as well as leggy or tapered vanities, to make rooms appear more spacious. To compensate for the loss of convenient storage, at one end of a counter add a cabinet for medicines, toiletries, and towels (above). If positioned correctly, a side cabinet can also screen the toilet (left).

RECESSED CABINETS Tucking in a cabinet between wall studs provides storage without taking up precious floor space. Shallow open shelves might display attractive bathroom items, such as soaps, guest towels, and pretty containers. A hinged door added to the recessed shelves can conceal not-so-attractive necessities. Translucent glass doors hinged to a recessed cabinet offer a happy compromise. The doors obscure neatly arranged towels at the top of the cabinet and easy-to-reach toiletries—organized in glass and metal containers—in the middle and bottom sections (below).

MEDICINE CABINETS One of the first things that comes to mind when thinking about bath storage is the medicine cabinet. It offers an easily accessible place to store numerous small items that are used frequently, such as medicines, vitamins, first-aid supplies, dental and hair products, and other items you prefer to keep out of the reach of small children. Today's medicine cabinets come in shapes, sizes, and styles to match any bath decor; some include towel racks, hooks, drawers, or pegs (above).

To add a touch of elegance to a bath, build a shallow cabinet the size of the inside measurement of a framed mirror, add adjustable glass shelves to the inside, attach the cabinet to the wall, and hinge the framed mirror onto the cabinet.

WALL CABINETS Storage of any kind is vital in baths with scant space. In large rooms, however, the best place for storage may not be directly above or below a sink. Cabinets with drawers and shelves, placed at a convenient level next to a sink or on an adjacent wall, offer the most accessible storage for regularly used items. A bank of wall cabinets has numerous spaces for shampoo, lotion, and bath toys (above).

Hang other useful wall cabinets above a tub to display decorative bottles or over a toilet to hide workaday items, such as toilet paper and cleaning supplies. Make sure that cabinets are above the head level of a seated person.

undercover helpers

THERE'S NO NEED TO GROPE around in your bathroom cabinets in search of that extra tube of toothpaste. Door-mounted hardware, pullouts, and lazy Susans work just as hard in the bathroom as in the kitchen. Slim racks mounted to the inside of a cabinet door conveniently hold small supplies. To easily reach storage space under the sink, add wire baskets or other pullouts that are installed with full-extension drawer slides or on their own special framework. Lazy Susans are storage-go-rounds that provide access to items in the far reaches of your cabinetry.

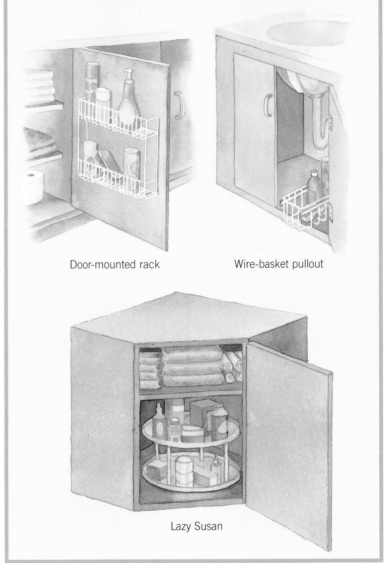

Door-mounted rack   Wire-basket pullout

Lazy Susan

HANG IT UP

When pedestal sinks and open vanities replace sink-topped cabinets, hanging storage takes up some of the slack. Well-placed hangers clear floor space and keep towels and robes easily accessible.

TOWEL HANGERS A row of hooks (right), bar-and-shelf combinations (below), stacked bars, and bars that swing back against the wall are all space-savers. Heated bars that double as radiators will keep towels toasty.

You can turn almost any attractive rack into a towel bar with some creativity. Wine racks can be converted into towel tidies, with a rolled-up towel fitting into each curved bottle holder. Adding two racks to a bathroom wall gives space for eight towels (below).

CHILD'S PLAY Attaching a peg-board to the bathroom door at a comfortable height for children provides a place for them to hang up clothes or to keep a woven basket that holds their towels and tub toys (right). Allot one peg per child and leave one or two free for extra items.

DOOR HANGERS Often, the back of the bathroom door yields overlooked storage space. Some retail hangers come with cubbies for stashing slippers, bath brushes, and towels. An over-the-door chrome and ceramic rack with multiple hooks adds instant hanging space for robes and towels (below).

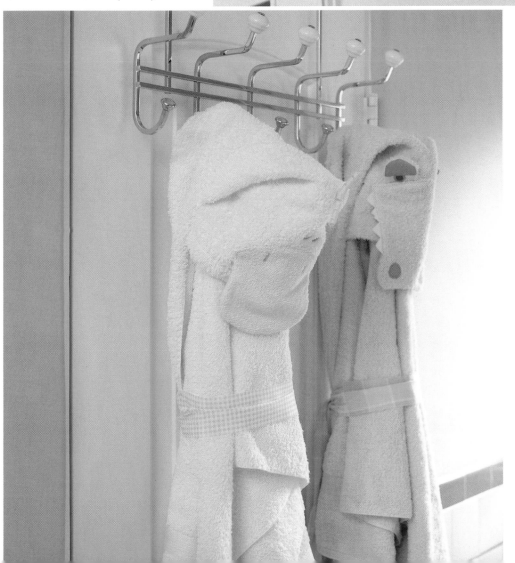

SHELF SMARTS

When dealing with tight spaces near a sink, shower, or tub, a shelf or two can make all the difference in how a bathroom functions. Versatile shelving is a prime space-saver and an inexpensive way to display towels, soaps, and other toiletries in often-overlooked areas. For example, a simple shelf mounted on brackets above a window adds unexpected storage. Open shelves fitted around one end of a bathtub hold towels within arm's reach (right). Shelves can also function as a decorative element, imparting a cozy, built-in feel to a utilitarian space.

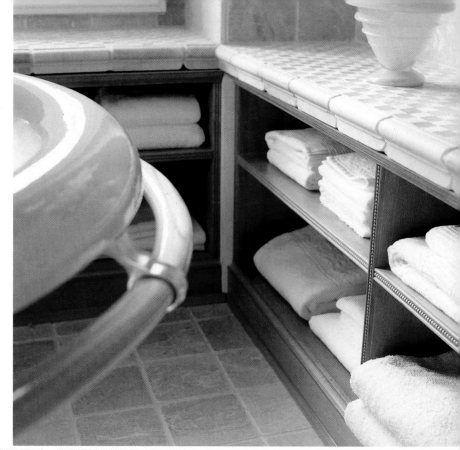

HARDWORKING SHELVES Often overlooked in modern bathrooms, shelves have great storage potential. Adding a sturdy yet inconspicuous glass shelf next to a bathtub gives you a spot for bath crystals and body scrubbers (above). A shelf with slots for cups that hold toothbrushes and toothpaste (left) is almost a necessity for sinks without a vanity or counter space.

DISAPPEARING SHELVES Now you see them—now you don't! To make a small bathroom appear more spacious, conceal built-in shelves behind a sliding door (right). The ledge over the sink holds only decorative items; bathroom essentials stay neatly hidden from view until the door is opened. Baskets, bowls, and a bucket round up toiletries and keep shelves organized.

BANJO COUNTER Extending a narrow shelf over the top of the toilet tank provides a longer surface for a small vanity and partially masks the toilet (below). And if the elements align, a banjo-shaped counter can extend beyond the toilet into the shower. This makes a small room appear larger and gives the shower a handy soap shelf.

STORING TOWELS OVERHEAD

Simple shelves built above the bathroom door provide extra storage for towels and supplies. To maximize space, roll towels rather than fold them.

FURNITURE ON ITS OWN

Bathroom furniture not only acts as storage but also personalizes the space. Recycled bureaus, sideboards, and wardrobes can create a look of the past; tansu cabinets can be adapted as artful vanities. Furniture made for bathroom use is smaller in scale than conventional furniture and uses finishes that stand up to humidity. If you introduce an old piece of furniture, be sure to treat it with a durable, moisture-proof finish.

TABLES If your bathroom lacks a vanity, bringing in a small table gives you a surface for storing bath products (above). And a tiered side table offers several layers of space on which to display attractive containers and toiletries (below).

HANDY HAMPERS Select a padded hamper (above) or a storage bench to keep laundry off the floor and to gain extra seating. Be sure that the hamper's lid comes equipped with safety hinges to avoid pinched fingers. When space is tight, choose a hamper that fits neatly in a corner. A removable liner makes it easy to tote laundry to the washing machine.

SEATING SPACE A stool, child's chair, or cube is a compact spot to stack towels (above) or reading material for leisure time in the bathtub; it also comes in handy when bathing tiny tots. If your bathroom has an open vanity, add a stool or chair as a convenience. Some rolling stools have a low shelf for storage.

PORTABLE CABINETS Choose a cabinet just the right size to fit neatly into a niche or nook of your bath. Or tuck a small cabinet on top of the vanity, beside an open vanity, between his-and-her vanities (right), or next to a shower. Models with doors or drawers will keep contents dust-free. Remember that frosted glass fronts mask contents, while clear glass offers a peek inside.

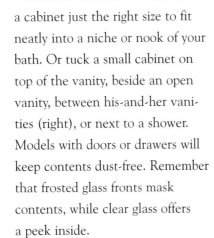

wood and water

DON'T WORRY ABOUT ADDING wooden furniture to a bathroom. Although hardwoods rarely were used in this humid environment in the past, today's durable finishes have made them handsome choices for bathroom cabinetry. Some hardwoods fare better than others in adapting to dampness; your best choices are ash, cherry, hickory, maple, oak, and walnut.

Manufacturers and installers apply finishes to new furniture and built-ins that keep moisture from penetrating the wood while still allowing it to expand and contract. If you're recycling an old wooden piece, protect it with a polyurethane finish or marine-type penetrating resin.

ORGANIZERS AND ACCESSORIES

Storing appliances and supplies where they are needed takes ingenuity, but handsome organizers help customize bathrooms. Interesting baskets, boxes, trunks, trays, bottles, and jars also add personality to what could be a sterile space (right).

VANITY INSERTS Slip plastic inserts into drawers to organize makeup and brushes (above). Special hinges can attach a molded tray inside the false drawer front of a vanity, creating room for toothbrushes and toothpaste. Plastic cups in adhesive holders fit flat against the inside of a medicine cabinet door to hold brushes, combs, and other items.

appliance adjuncts

AMONG THE HOST OF STORAGE AIDS designed for storing small bathroom appliances are wall- or door-mounted vinyl pouches (sold as closet organizers) and wire racks and baskets. If grooming appliances have hanging loops, use wall racks with hooks or pegs; or screw cup hooks to the underside of a shelf. To keep from damaging power cords, don't wrap them around appliances. Instead, coil cords into loose loops and stuff them into empty bathroom tissue tubes. Always wait until appliances are cool before putting them away.

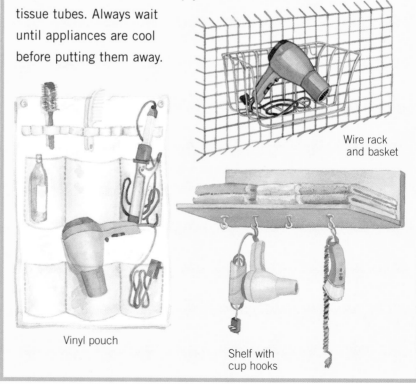

Wire rack and basket

Vinyl pouch

Shelf with cup hooks

BATH CATCHALLS A generous caddy slipped over the showerhead holds soaps and shampoos. Some models add hooks for washcloths, scrub brushes, and loofah sponges. A caddy that you slide over the top of the tub keeps bath salts, soaps, and lotions at hand. Tucking shower essentials—and tub toys—into the small pockets of a plastic shower curtain makes it easy to grab what's needed (right).

TISSUE TIDIES You'll always know when it's time to buy more when you place a generous wicker basket or a covered hamper beside the toilet to hold extra tissue rolls (right). A hamper can also conceal other personal hygiene products.

ORGANIZER WALL In a bath without a vanity, a room divider becomes a wall of storage (left). To make the best use of the space, the sizes of the open-topped wicker organizers determine the proportions of the cabinet housing them. Grouping similar baskets in a variety of sizes lets you cluster towels, toiletries, cosmetics, appliances, and other bath items without having a clutter of containers.

chapter five

other spaces

Utilitarian spaces, such as home offices, laundry rooms, and mudrooms, merit great organizational attention when you consider how often they're used. A little planning can turn these hardworking zones from centers of clutter to models of efficiency. The rooms can even serve multiple functions, which is essential when space is tight.

Garages, attics, and basements are the ideal places for all those things that you use seasonally, put aside for the future, or can't fit anywhere else. These spaces can be organized so that they provide all the extra storage that you need. Since they are not formal living areas, they don't have to look fancy and can be outfitted rather inexpensively with a variety of storage options.

Take advantage of these great areas by storing everything so that it can be found easily, without having to disrupt the rest of these rooms.

home offices

The key to creating an efficient office, whether it is separate from the rest of the house or tucked into a room that serves another purpose, is to start with good, basic office furniture. The home-office market has grown considerably, and there are modular systems and stand-alone pieces of furniture to fit any scenario.

WORKING IN BORROWED SPACE

When you set up your office in a room used for other purposes, the most important principle is to blend the work space with its surroundings and to keep it free of office clutter. This is not as difficult as it sounds if you choose the right pieces for your work area. For example, if you are adding a workstation to your kitchen or great room, check out cabinets that come with matching desks and wall shelves (top, right).

OFFICE ARMOIRES One of the best ways to disguise your office completely is to enclose it within an armoire or cabinet (right), which can be purchased to suit almost any interior decor. The doors open to expose a desk surface, keyboard tray, file space, and bookshelves. Some are equipped with a shelf under the desktop for storing a CPU. Armoires and cabinets are a bit limited for a full-scale business operation but provide the storage needed for telecommuting and household management.

CLOSET OPTIONS When you are carving out space for an office in a guest room, consider hiding your desk inside the closet (right). A 24-inch-deep closet is well suited for this purpose. The only modification you may have to make is to add an electrical outlet. Start with a stock desktop; these are available in sizes ranging from 20 to 36 inches deep and 28 to 70 inches long. Customize the space with a keyboard tray, shelving, a file cabinet, letter boxes, and a message board.

CREATIVE FILING One limitation of having an office in a dual-use room is that it is difficult to find a place for the invaluable but often unattractive file cabinet. You can buy file cabinets that are disguised as furniture—footstools, side tables, and rattan or wooden boxes—to match your room's style (below).

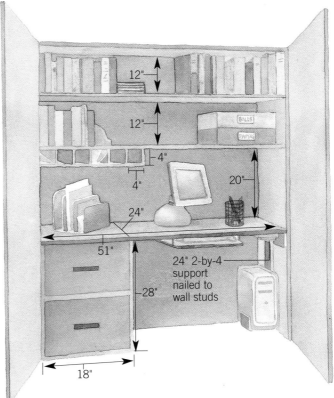

OFFICE IN A CLOSET

Create an office in an empty reach-in closet with only a file cabinet, a desktop, and bookshelves. When you're finished working, you can shut the doors and your office is completely hidden.

EVERYTHING IN ITS PLACE

If you develop a smart organizational system in your office for supplies and equipment, they will be easy to find. Since the market for home-office organizing products is growing, you can find storage for every type of office accessory in every style imaginable. Keeping your office as stylish as the rest of your house is important, since you may spend more time there than anywhere else.

DESKTOP ORGANIZERS Desktop trays and letter organizers come in both horizontal and vertical styles and in such materials as metal mesh, wire, galvanized steel, plastic, rattan, wood (below), colored cardboard, and even leather. Some organizers combine horizontal trays with vertical slots so that you can store paper, mail, and file folders in the same spot; some include small holders for pens, paper clips, and business cards.

DESKTOP HUTCHES Placing a hutch on your desk gives you space to keep paperwork and small items organized and off your desktop without having to attach something to the wall. Many have space for files and stationery (above). Most hutches are no deeper than the width of a sheet of paper—about 9 inches—leaving room in front of them on the desktop to work.

PEN CANISTERS An attractive addition to your desktop is a pen holder with individual slots that keep writing utensils at your fingertips (top, right, facing page). If you want to add a little color to the room, find a bright coffee mug to serve this purpose.

CDs AND DISKS CD and computer disk storage is available in many styles, from holders that sit on your desktop (near right) to those that mount on a wall. If your office needs a little pizzazz, look for CD holders in bright colors and unusual shapes.

DRAWER DIVIDERS A great way to separate pens, tape, sticky pads, paper clips, staples, and all the other items you store in a desk drawer is to add dividers. Some drawers come with inserts and dividers, but you can also use anything from loaf pans (below) to small open boxes.

MAGAZINE BUTLERS You can hold up to a year's worth of periodicals in a magazine butler (right) so individual issues are easy to find and won't fall over on your bookshelf. The least expensive come in colored cardboard, but you can find others in materials to match the rest of your office accessories.

CONTAINERS Available in all sizes and in materials ranging from sturdy cardboard (above) to rattan to galvanized metal, fashionable containers organize such supplies as colored paper, paints, pens, files, and anything else you might store in your office. Purchase stackable containers that fit below your desk, on your bookshelves, or in a closet.

laundry rooms

Lose the laundry blues by organizing the washing and drying space into sorting, folding, and ironing centers, each equipped with supplies necessary to perform the task. Key elements include ample storage for detergent; a utility sink for items that need washing by hand; a rack or clothesline for drip-drying; a table or 36-inch-high counter for folding; water-resistant, easy-to-clean work surfaces; and adequate task lighting.

LAUNDRY 101

Utilize space above, below, beside, and between the washer and dryer. Some new models come with a storage drawer below the machine (top, right). Provide plenty of storage accessories for sorting, hooks for hanging, shelves for stacking (below), and laundry caddies for transporting clothes. Add a step-on can for disposing of lint, a see-through container for items retrieved from pockets, and a bulletin board for tacking up laundry-care tags.

HIDING THE LAUNDRY When a washer and dryer are tucked into an alcove, add shelves, wall cabinets, or cubbies for supplies. Cover it all up with easy-to-open bifold, sliding, or pocket doors, or with seamless cabinet doors that offer access to each area independently. If a front-loading pair—either side by side or stacked—are nestled into a cabinet run, mask them with doors that match their surroundings (above). Adjacent cabinets or drawers might house an ironing board, pull-out sorting table, and tilt-down clothes bin.

SUPPLIES Store laundry supplies together on a shelf or in a cabinet near the washer and dryer so that they can be retrieved and replaced easily. As they are necessities, not accessories, it is neater to hide them in a cabinet rather than display them on a shelf. If you don't have that option, coralling supplies in attractive containers on shelves will keep them organized and easy to reach (below). If space is at a premium, consider a pull-out caddy that fits between the washer and dryer (left). Where cabinetry is scarce, add a freestanding organizer, such as a series of wire shelves.

HANGING AND FOLDING When clothes are dry, hang them up or smooth and fold them right away. Save ironing time by hanging garments that easily wrinkle on a rod as soon as they are taken from the dryer. Counters (left) and shelves are better places to fold clothes than the top of a washer or dryer. Even a collapsible shelf over the appliances maximizes vertical space; just flip it down when needed and flip it up when not in use. Some roll-around laundry racks are equipped with flip-down folding counters and hanging rods. Stack clean and folded laundry on shelves or place clothes in each family member's portable container.

Once dirty clothes are collected and sorted, washing them becomes a cinch. Ideally, family members should carry their own laundry to and from the washer and dryer. Portable receptacles placed in their bedrooms or baths remind them of the chore (left).

BUILT-IN SORTER

One option for sorting clothes is to build a cabinet with a single deep drawer under a counter. Use plywood dividers to partition the drawer into compartments for whites, colors, and permanent press. Another divider could be added for towels and sheets. Install the drawer with heavy-duty drawer slides.

Pull-out bins (above), hampers, or baskets in the laundry room encourage family members to separate clothes. Label or color-code hampers for lights and darks. If you have the space, add organizers for such items as hand-washables and permanent-press garments.

IRONING CENTER An iron and a full-size ironing board that pulls down for use might be stored inside a wall-mounted or recessed cabinet (above). If the cabinet is equipped with a light and an electrical outlet for the iron, make sure there is a safety switch to cut power when the door is closed. If you're short on space, choose an ironing board that hangs over a door. Boards come with an array of chic covers, but solids make it easier to see wrinkles.

LAUNDRY CHUTE A built-in laundry chute transports clothing from an upper floor down to a laundry room. A pull-out hamper is situated underneath the end of the chute to catch clothing as it drops through (right). When it's time to put in a load of laundry, the hamper rolls easily over to the washing machine.

where to locate a laundry chute

A LAUNDRY CHUTE directs dirty clothes from your home's main or second floor to a laundry center in the basement or garage below. You can locate the chute opening in an inconspicuous but handy spot: inside a clothes closet in the master bedroom; in a wall, with a hinged or flap door; or inside a bathroom cabinet. To reduce the risk of small children falling into the chute, be sure that the opening is raised high above the floor and measures no more than 12 inches across.

The best time to construct your chute is when you're designing or remodeling your house. Build the chute from sheet aluminum, 18-inch-diameter furnace heating duct, or plywood, depending on your local building codes.

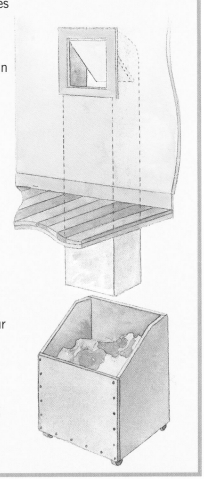

mudrooms

A laundry room often shares space with a mudroom. This family loading and unloading zone near the back or side door probably sees more in-and-out traffic than the front entry. Everyone stops here at least long enough to park book bags, shed dirty shoes, and drop off tennis racquets. When outfitted with carefully planned storage systems, effective mudrooms neatly capture back-door clutter and much more.

BENCHES, RACKS, AND SHELVES Instead of letting a mudroom become cluttered, take advantage of its potential. Counters, tables, and benches are storage pieces that collect and organize both day-to-day and seasonal items. When outfitted with a bench surrounded by four generously sized cubbies, a makeshift mudroom area near the back door efficiently stores jackets, purses, and dog leashes, as well as extra bags of dog food (below).

Many cost-effective storage solutions are tailored specially for utility spaces. You'll find a wealth of inexpensive organizing aids, such as wall-mounted racks for boots (top, right), shelves for shoes, and hangers for coats (below, right), in catalogs and at home centers and container stores.

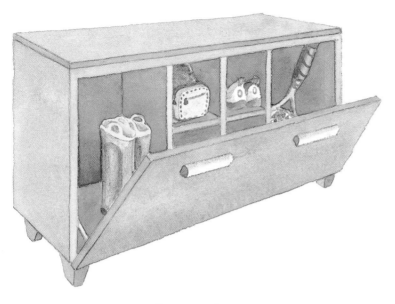

CATCHALL CABINET

When a utility space opens onto a deck, patio, or yard, shoes and gardening gear tend to pile up by the door. An easy-to-make drop-front cabinet helps control the mess. The cubbies are suitable for extra boots, book bags, or bulky outdoor items.

PET LOCKER If you need more than just a hook for Fido's leashes, build a small closet with a hinged door to hide your pet's necessities (above). Divide the interior into compartments for essentials, such as food, shampoo, medications, and toys. Add hooks for collars, leashes, brushes, and combs; also consider a rod to hold a roll of pickup bags. A freestanding box could also round up feeding bowls, food, towels, and toys. For convenience, locate the closet near a laundry sink where your pet may at least tolerate a bath.

LOCKER ROOM Adding a built-in wall cabinet is one of the best ways to organize an active family's sports clothing and gear, hats, jackets, shoes, pool towels, and the like (left). Add a pull-out rod for hanging wet clothes and an accompanying bench or stool for unloading bags or changing shoes.

garages, attics, and basements

I n many a garage, attic, or basement, the most accessible objects are those that were last deposited. This is a recipe for chaos, making it impossible to find anything quickly. When rearranging your space, separate items into current storage, seasonal, and long-term categories. Then dedicate a place within easy reach for items you use regularly, such as dry goods, foods, sporting equipment, and tools.

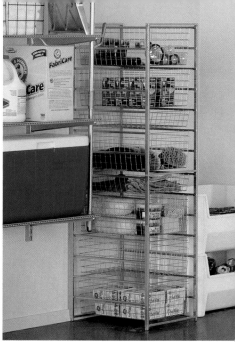

DRY GOODS AND FOODS

Buying dry goods and foods in bulk saves both time and money. But finding a place to store the oversize boxes of cereal, the flats of canned goods, and the giant containers of detergent presents a problem. You want to reach these without pushing anything else aside. Store them close to the door, either on open shelves or in cabinets, keeping heavier items between waist and chest height (left). If you store such bulk goods as flour and sugar, use large plastic containers with secure lids to keep moisture, insects, and rodents out.

TIERED RACKS If you keep a supply of canned goods in this area, use tiered racks or risers on your shelves for easy identification (left).

STACKING BINS AND WIRE DRAWERS Use metal frames with stacking bins or wire drawers in conjunction with shelving to organize a garage or basement wall for dry goods and foods (top).

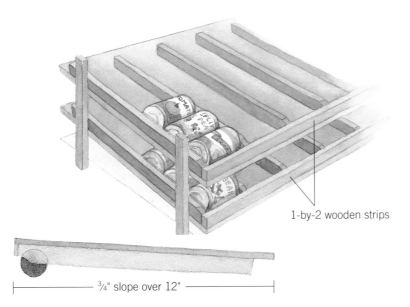

1-by-2 wooden strips

¾" slope over 12"

SLOPING SHELVES FOR CAN STORAGE

Food shelves that hold only bulk canned goods can be sloped forward so that cans will roll to the front, saving you the trouble of digging for buried cans. Fasten 1-by-2 strips across the front and sides of the shelves to form channels that keep cans aligned, as shown above. Make the channels ⅛-inch wider than the height of the cans you're storing and, if possible, leave the back of the shelves accessible for loading. The shelves should slope ¾ inch for every 12 inches of shelf depth.

RECYCLING BINS Recycling bins are now commonly kept in kitchen cabinets, but if you don't have space in your kitchen, create a recycling station in your garage. The containers should be easily accessible to toss in materials and lightweight enough to carry out to the curb on collection day.

Keep bins in a well-ventilated area, since even rinsed-out cans and bottles can smell. Alternatively, many communities now collect all recyclable materials—paper, glass, plastic, and aluminum—together. In that case, you can use one large garbage can.

If you need to separate the materials, try using stackable plastic bins placed on the floor or on a shelving system (top, right). Attach casters to the bottoms of plastic bins or wooden crates to give them mobility.

(You can buy sets of wheels that simply snap on the bottoms of some recycle bins.) To keep several bins together, build a wooden crate to hold them. If you want to hide your recycling, install one or two slide-out undercounter garbage pails inside the bottom of a wall cabinet with doors.

HANGING RECYCLING BINS

If you have the wall space, hang plastic recycling bins one above the other on sets of angle iron brackets, cut to length and reinforced with diagonal braces bolted in place (left). The bins should easily slide in and out of the assembly. Keep in mind that the bins will be rather heavy when full, so be sure to hang them only from a solid wall, such as one made of plywood or masonry; or use bins whose width corresponds to the spacing of the studs.

99

SPORTING EQUIPMENT

Sporting equipment should be stored so that it can be easily reached. A manufactured garage wall rack system can be outfitted with baskets and hooks to hold almost any kind of equipment, but with a little ingenuity and enough wall or ceiling space, you can build your own. Metal shelving on tracks (right) or Peg-Board secured to the wall is a convenient place to hang lightweight sporting equipment, such as tennis rackets and bike helmets, from rubberized S-shaped hooks.

BALLS   A wooden bin, a tall wire basket, or an open cardboard box keeps inflated basketballs and soccer balls under control in the garage. Where floor space is limited, store balls in a laundry bag hanging from a hook on the wall (below) or in a lightweight wire basket hung from a peg. Store balls for children at their shoulder height or lower.

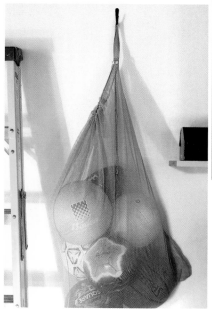

GOLF EQUIPMENT   Keep your golf bags off the floor and your golf shoes nearby on a wall-hanging rack (above). If you don't play frequently, store the bag in a cabinet or in a storage loft overhead.

TENNIS GEAR   Hang rackets on hooks and store accessories on shelves (above). If you hang rackets on pegs, place two pegs about a neck width apart and rest the racket's face on top of them.

BICYCLES One of the hardest items to accommodate is a bicycle, especially if you have more than one. Manufactured bike racks include wall-hanging and stand-alone types, as well as floor-to-ceiling poles. There is even a ceiling rack that includes a pulley system for easy raising and lowering (above). For very little money, though, you can create a wall rack on which multiple bikes hang vertically, using a 2-by-4 runner board and rubberized J-shaped hooks.

HORIZONTAL BIKE HANGER

To hang a single bike, nail two closet rod brackets side by side into the wall studs so that the half-round notches hold the bike's crossbar.

SPECIALTY RACKS You can purchase a specialty rack to hold odd-sized sporting equipment, such as hockey sticks and kayak oars. If you have fishing gear, hang poles along the wall with S-shaped hooks or in a rod rack (above); or suspend them horizontally from the ceiling. A tackle box is best kept on a shelf.

SNOW AND WATER EQUIPMENT

Use L-shaped hooks on Peg-Board or attached to the wall for storing snowboards, wakeboards, and surfboards (below).

A manufactured ski rack will hold skis, poles, and boots all in one place (below, right). If you don't have the wall space, store skis and boards vertically in a shallow cabinet or horizontally suspended from the ceiling or on a storage loft. Boots should be kept in a cloth or paper bag to keep them from gathering dust and spiders.

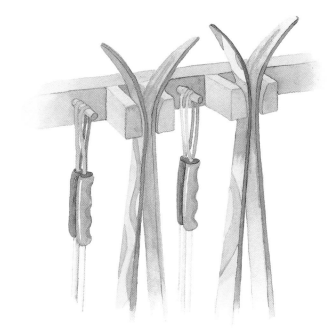

BLOCK-AND-PEG SKI RACK

With their curved tips, skis are easy to hang between blocks. Make a simple rack by fixing a pair of wooden blocks to a 2-by-4 runner board for every set of skis and fastening the runner along a wall. Drill pilot holes in 2-by-4 blocks and then attach the blocks to the runner with glue and screws. Space the blocks 1¼ inch apart, rounding over and sanding their inside edges to follow the profile of the skis and prevent scratching them. Ski poles can be hung on pegs glued into holes drilled into the runner.

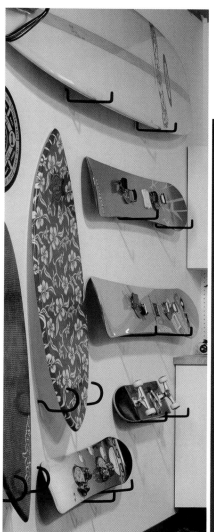

WORKSHOPS

When setting up your workshop, the most important quality is accessibility. The best-equipped workshop functions poorly if items are disorganized or hard to reach. An efficient workshop also needs good lighting and ventilation, as well as an energy source next to the work area (top, right).

WORKBENCHES   Critical to any functional workshop is a sturdy workbench. Many workbenches incorporate cabinets, drawers, hutches, and backboards (below and right). If you need a larger surface or want to create your own workbench, place a 2-foot-wide length of lumber or a flat door on top of old kitchen base cabinets or on a bathroom vanity. Hang old kitchen wall cabinets above the workbench. If you don't have old cabinets, ask local contractors for discards from kitchen remodels. The cabinet drawers and shelves provide great storage for tools and various accessories.

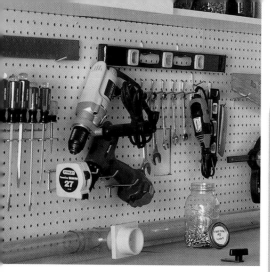

TOOL STORAGE Line the wall behind your workbench with Peg-Board and use it to hang hand tools from hooks (above). If it's a challenge for you to keep the board organized, you can make paper profiles of your tools and glue them to the board, providing a designated spot for each tool.

Small tools or such items as drill bits can be organized in a wooden or plastic utensil tray and stored on top of the workbench or in drawers in a tool chest (below). Large tools, such as electric sanders, drills, and routers, can be stored in the same tool chest or on shelves in cabinets below the workbench.

finding a place for lumber

MOST DO-IT-YOURSELF HOME OWNERS have a few pieces of wood saved from previous jobs. If you have enough wall space, you can create horizontal storage for lumber using metal tracks with brackets (below). If your walls are exposed, use the space between the wall studs to stack lumber vertically; secure the lumber to the wall with wood or rubber straps.

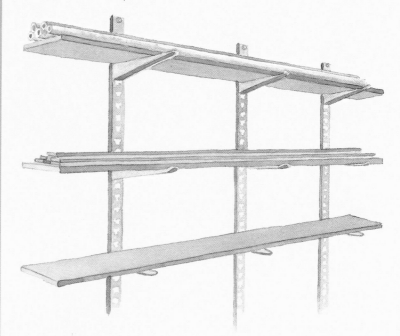

Don't forget the space up high. The area just above the top of the garage door is ideal for a long shelf. If an attic or garage ceiling is left open, the space between the ceiling joists or above open rafters is ideal for storing long, thin materials, such as lumber or pipes (below).

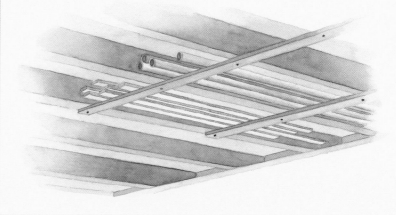

NAIL AND SCREW STORAGE

Finding the right-size nails can be a chore. Divide nails by size and keep them in labeled plastic containers or glass jars on shelves (below, right) or in drawers. If you store nails in glass jars, you can screw the lids to the underside of a shelf or cabinet and then screw the jars into the lids (right).

You can also purchase a plastic storage box with bins made specifically for hardware (below, left) or use a drawer organizer with multiple compartments to store nails and screws by size.

HANGING JARS UNDER A SHELF

Mounting jars under a shelf will double its storage capacity. Fasten the jar lids to the shelf with screws and washers and then screw the jars to the lids.

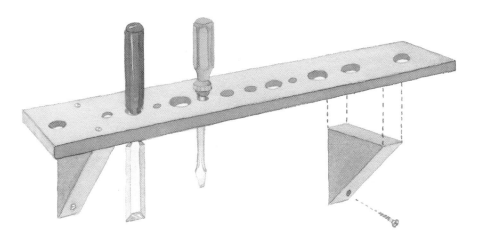

WALL-MOUNTED TOOL RACK

Drill holes through a length of 1-by-4 lumber and attach it to the wall with wooden braces to hold tools, such as screwdrivers and chisels.

SEASONAL AND LONG-TERM STORAGE

Items you don't use frequently or are saving for a rainy day can be stored out of normal reach—either high on shelves, suspended from the ceiling, or under the basement stairs. However, you should still be able to locate and access them easily. Anything stored long term should be labeled and protected in bags or containers against moisture, dust, rodents, and insects.

HOLIDAY DECORATIONS   How often have you purchased new decorations because you forgot where you stored the ones from the year before? The best way to organize them is to put them in labeled plastic or cardboard boxes—a different one for each holiday you celebrate. The toughest things to store safely are blown eggs and tree ornaments and lights.

Blown eggs can be placed in cardboard egg boxes. And you can store ornaments in their original boxes or in specialty ornament boxes with individual compartments that protect them from breakage (top, right). Keep lights untangled by wrapping them around a large sheet of cardboard notched with Vs or a large cardboard tube; then store them in a flat plastic box (above). The following year you can unroll the lights from the board or tube as you walk around the tree. Wrap such items as menorahs, statues, and holiday serving pieces in cotton sheeting, old towels, or tissue paper; then place them in boxes. Stack the boxes on shelves (right) or in labeled trunks or bins.

CAMPING EQUIPMENT Most camping equipment—such as tents, sleeping bags, stoves, collapsible chairs, and coolers—stacks easily and is light enough to store up high. Keep it on the upper shelves of cabinets or a wall system. Manufactured wire shelves can be suspended from a high ceiling (left). Or create a loft shelf, either suspended from the ceiling joists or tucked above open rafters.

overhead storage

MANY GARAGES AND ATTICS have high or open ceilings that provide a place for extra storage, either suspended from the joists or built between the joists and rafters. Since you may need a ladder to access this area, you should only store things here that are used infrequently and are light enough to lift down easily. Empty suitcases, lightweight camping gear, seasonal sporting equipment, and cushions from patio furniture can all be stored overhead.

In a garage or attic that is open between the joists and rafters, straddle items on the rafters or set sheets of plywood on top of the rafters to create overhead shelving.

If the space has a flat ceiling, you can build in suspended shelving using 2-by-4 stock and plywood (right). Assemble two or more sets of wooden racks with lag screws or bolts, making sure they are wide enough to support a shelf (3 feet is a good distance). The length of the verticals depends on the height of your ceiling and the amount of clearance you need. Bolt the uprights of each rack to a joist. Racks should be no more than 4 feet apart. Nail a sheet of plywood on top of two or more racks to create the shelf.

SPACE ABOVE JOISTS

In many garages there is usable storage space between the joists or collar beams overhead and the rafters. This space provides a ready-to-use storage place for your seasonal items.

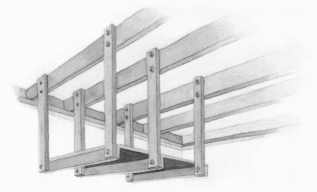

SUSPENDED SHELVES

U-shaped racks made from 2-by-4 stock and attached to ceiling joists are handy for long-term storage.

CLOTHING Out-of-season outfits and children's outgrown clothing often make their way to the attic or basement. If you store clothing in fabric garment bags, be sure to hang clothes on wooden hangers rather than wire ones. Hang garment bags from closet rods that are fastened between the rafters in an attic or from furring strips screwed across the ceiling joists in a basement or insulated garage. (Never bore holes through joists for the rods.) You can also set up a collapsible hanging rod in an unused corner (right).

The ideal solution is to line a freestanding or built-in wardrobe with cedar and store hanging bags inside. Folded clothes should be wrapped in tissue before being placed in cedar-lined trunks or boxes. Clothing should always be clean and stored in a dry area; excessive dampness creates mold.

QUILTS, BLANKETS, AND LINENS
Fold or roll linens; then wrap them in clean cotton pillowcases or sheets or in layers of tissue paper, never in plastic. Then store them overhead or in trunks (left). Quilts and linens should be taken out of their cases and refolded at least once a year to prevent creases from discoloring. Woolen blankets should be preserved with mothballs or stored in cedar chests.

By law you are required to save your tax records for at least three years after you file your taxes. Keep them in cardboard document boxes (left). Property and other investment records need to be held indefinitely. The best way to do this is to store your records in file folders and keep them in acid- and lignin-free document boxes. The boxes can be stacked high on shelves or above the rafters. If you have sufficient floor space, you can also store records in old vertical file cabinets you can buy cheaply at a used-office-furniture store or at a garage sale.

firewood

THE GARAGE IS A GOOD PLACE to shelter firewood from the elements. But keeping it contained can be a challenge. Whether your wood is dry and seasoned or recently cut, it must be kept from ground moisture and stored so that air can circulate around it. Wood can be stacked in either parallel or perpendicular (crisscross) rows. Store a pile of wood under the basement stairs off the floor or in an open cabinet in the garage. Metal firewood holders with side supports also hold a good supply of wood indoors.

Firewood can become infested with anything from ants to wood beetles. Minimize or prevent this problem by keeping the wood off the ground. Never store wood up against the outside of your house, as insects can make their way inside through cracks in the foundation. (If you're storing wood outside, keep it at least 10 feet from the wall, if possible.) Bang each piece of wood against the ground to dislodge as many insects as possible before you bring it inside.

To reduce the risk of insects' spreading in the house, only bring in wood as you need it; in general, don't store more than a few days' worth of wood inside. As an additional precaution, you can surround the inside firewood bin with sticky glue strips to catch any insects that wander away from the woodpile. Glue strips are more effective than bait traps, which actually attract certain kinds of insects.

resource guide

STORAGE AND ORGANIZATION PRODUCT RETAILERS

CALIFORNIA CLOSETS
1-800-274-6754
www.calclosets.com.

THE CONTAINER STORE
1-888-266-8246
www.containerstore.com

HOLD EVERYTHING
1-800-421-2264
www.holdeverything.com

ORGANIZED LIVING
1-800-862-6556

ORGANIZE-EVERYTHING.COM
1-800-600-9817
www.organize-everything.com

ORGANIZE-IT
1-800-210-7712
www.organizes-it.com

STACKS AND STACKS HOMEWARES
1-800-761-5222
www.stacksandstacks.com

HOME FURNISHING RETAILERS

CRATE & BARREL
1-800-967-6696
www.crateandbarrel.com

IKEA
1-800-434-4532
www.ikea-usa.com

POTTERY BARN
1-888-779-5176
www.potterybarn.com

RESTORATION HARDWARE
1-800-762-1005
www.restorationhardware.com

ONLINE AND CATALOG RESOURCES

ARCHIVAL METHODS
1-866-877-7050
www.archivalmethods.com

BALLARD DESIGNS
1-800-367-2775
www.ballarddesigns.com

BERKELEY MILLS
1-510-549-2854
www.berkeleymills.com

COCOON
1-800-842-4352
www.cocoononline.com

DESIGN WITHIN REACH
1-800-944-2233
www.dwr.com

EASY TRACK
1-800-562-4257
www.easytrack.com

EXPOSURES
1-800-222-4947
www.exposuresonline.com

FRENCH COUNTRY LIVING
1-800-743-7732
www.frenchcountryliving.com

FRONTGATE
1-888-263-9850
www.frontgate.com

GEMPLER'S
1-800-382-8473
www.gemplers.com

GOOD CATALOG
www.goodcatalog.com

THE HOME MARKETPLACE
1-800-356-3876
www.thehomemarketplace.com

HYLOFT USA, LLC
1-866-249-5638
www.hyloftusa.com

IMPROVEMENTS
1-800-642-2112
www.improvementscatalog.com

THE MUSEUM OF MODERN ART
1-800-793-3167
www.moma.org

THE MUSEUM OF USEFUL THINGS STORE
1-800-515-2707
www.themut.com

PALOS SPORTS
1-800-233-5484
www.palossports.com

RACOR
1-800-783-7725
www.racorinc.com

SHARPER IMAGE
1-800-344-5555
www.sharperimage.com

SINCERELY YOURS
1-800-297-4860
www.sincerelyyours.com

SOLUTIONS
1-877-718-7901
www.solutionscatalog.com

CHILDREN'S RESOURCES

CHILDCRAFT
1-800-631-5652
www.childcraft.com

POTTERY BARN KIDS
1-800-993-4923
www.potterybarnkids.com

MEMBERSHIP WAREHOUSE CLUBS

COSTCO
1-800-774-2678
www.costco.com

SAM'S CLUB
1-800-925-6278
www.samsclub.com

WOODWORKING & HARDWARE RESOURCES

A BIG WAREHOUSE
1-480-892-7818
www.abigwarehouse.com

ROCKLER
1-800-279-4441
www.rockler.com

VAN DYKE'S RESTORERS
1-800-787-3355
www.vandykes.com

KITCHEN CABINET AND HARDWARE MANUFACTURERS & SUPPLIERS

BOWERY KITCHEN SUPPLY
1-212-376-4982
www.bowerykitchens.com

BULTHAUP KITCHEN ARCHITECTURE
New York: 1-212-966-7183
www.bulthaup.com

HÄFELE
1-800-423-3531
www.hafeleonline.com/usa

KITCHEN ACCESSORIES UNLIMITED
1-800-667-8721
www.kitchenaccessoriesunlimited.com

KRAFTMAID
1-800-571-1990
www.kraftmaid.com

REAL SOLUTIONS FOR REAL LIFE BY KNAPE & VOGT
1-616-459-3311
www.knapeandvogt.com

REV-A-SHELF
1-800-626-1126
www.rev-a-shelf.com

RUBBERMAID
1-330-264-6464
1-888-895-2110
www.rubbermaid.com

SIEMATIC
1-215-244-6800
www.siematic.com

ACKNOWLEDGMENTS

We would like to thank the following people and businesses for their assistance: Fray Below; Thomas Blaine; Carrie Bowman, Amy Kirkbride, and Bill Larsen, Knape & Vogt; Bulthaup; Keri Butler, Rubbermaid; Beate Chelette, Beateworks; Amy Crowley and Lauren Henderson, Frontgate; Lois Erbay and Jan Schlesinger, California Closets; Stacey Fischer, Exposures; Frank Gaglione; Gloria Gale; Bette Johnson, Windquest Companies Inc.; the library staff at SPC Picture Collection; Holly Logsdon and Diane Rock, Rev-A-Shelf; Tim Matthias, HyLoft USA, LLC; Carolyn McMannam and Kelly Vrtis, The Container Store; Joan Perniconi, Crate & Barrel; Debbie Schwartz, The Village Collection Inc.; Janice Simonsen, IKEA; Marion and Fred Sotcher; Thomas J. Story; Annie Terracciano, Racor, Inc.

credits

PHOTOGRAPHERS

Jean Allsopp/SPC Picture Collection: 48 left, 62 right, 65 top left; Dennis Anderson: 36 bottom right; Ron Anderson: 39 top left; Jim Bathie: cover, 66 left; Ed Caldwell: 75 right; James Carrier: 19 bottom right, 42 top, 78 bottom right, 86; Ken Chen: 103 top right; Crandall & Crandall: 50 top left; Crate & Barrel/James Baigrie: 19 top right, 90 left; Crate & Barrel/Steven McDonald: 51 top right; Crate & Barrel/Simon Watson: 22 bottom left, 31 bottom right; Crate & Barrel/Gintas Zaranka: 90 left; Grey Crawford: 43 top right; Frank Gaglione: 71 left; Lauren W. Glenn/SPC Picture Collection: 48 bottom right; Tria Giovan: 6, 19 left, 28, 39 bottom left, 45 left, 79 top, 81 top, 83 top left; Jay Graham: 31 top, 40 bottom right, 41 left, 46 top right; John Granen: 80 top, 83 top right, 92 top right; Ken Gutmaker: 13 left, 47 bottom right, 57 right, 92 bottom right; Jamie Hadley: 37 left, 43 bottom right; Margot Hartford: 8 top right; Philip Harvey: 48 top right, 49 top right, 95 left; Michael Jensen: 45 top right; Douglas Johnson: 74 left; Steve Keating: 78 bottom left; Muffy Kibbey: 80 bottom right, 96 left; Dennis Krukowski: 82 bottom; David Duncan Livingston: 39 top right, 73 left, 94 right; Kathryn MacDonald: 50 bottom; Peter Malinowski/InSite: 38 right; Dave Marlow: 74 right; Sylvia Martin/SPC Picture Collection: 20 bottom right; E. Andrew McKinney: 23 bottom right, 56 left, 69 all, 72 top right, 73 left, 88 bottom; Susan Gentry McWhinney: 58, 67 top; Art Meripol/SPC Picture Collection: 57 top left; Miller/Stein Design: 46 left; Kit Morris: 24 top right, 51 left, 82 top right; Wendy Nordeck: 81 bottom; David Papazian: 44 top left, 89 top; David Phelps: 29 bottom left; Norman A. Plate: 36 left, 106 bottom right; David Prince: 3 bottom, 4 left and bottom right, 10 top and bottom right, 30 right, 57 bottom left, 65 top, 84 right, 85 top, 90 top right, 91 bottom left, 96 right; Tom Rider: 33; Brad Simmons/Beateworks.com: 7; Michael Skott: 12 right, 13 top right, 17 bottom right, 18 left, 22 top left, 23 left and top right, 29 top, 32, 37 bottom right, 42 bottom, 51 bottom right, 83 bottom right; Thomas J. Story: 4 top right, 8 left, 9 center, 12 left, 13 top right, 26 bottom, 30 bottom left, 41 top right, 52 all, 53 top and bottom left, 54, 56 top and bottom right, 67 bottom left, 72 left and bottom right, 73 bottom right, 76 right, 78 top, 79 bottom, 82 top left, 84 left, 93 top and bottom left, 97 right, 98 left, 100 left, 101 left, 104 all, 105 all, 106 left and top right, 108 top, 109; Tim Street-Porter: 45 bottom right, 71 top right; Tim Street-Porter/Beateworks.com: 15, 16 bottom, 34, 40 top right, 43 left; Brian Vanden Brink: 11, 17 top right, 22, 24 bottom right, 29 bottom right, 44 right, 59, 67 bottom right, 91 bottom right, 92 left, 97 left, 108 bottom; Michal Venera: 8 bottom right, 9 top right, 14, 16 top, 17 left, 20 left, 31 bottom left, 76 left, 89 bottom left, 94 left; Jessie Walker: 38 top left, 47 bottom left, 66 right; David Wakely: 3, 24 left, 37 top right, 39 bottom right, 41 bottom right, 46 bottom right, 85 bottom, 88 top, 95 right; Laurey Weigent: page 48 bottom right, page 72 bottom left; Ben Woolsey: 47 top right

ARCHITECTS & DESIGNERS

Andre Rothblatt Architecture: 47 bottom right, 57 right; Arkin-Tilt Architects: 75 top right; Associates III/Cottle Graybeal Yaw Architects: 74 right; Patricia Bainter: 37 top right; Bernhard & Priestly Architects: 24 top right; BurksToma Architects, Marie Fisher Interior Design, Min/Day: 40 bottom right; C. David Robinson Architects: 76 right; Susan Christman: 47 top right; City Building, Inc: 49 top right; Butch Cleveland: 103 top right; Custom Electronics Designers: 17 top right; Nancy Cowall Cutler: 56 left; Malcolm Davis: 50 bottom; Jean-Louis Deniot: 45 left; Donham & Sweeny Architects: 67 bottom right; Sasha Dunn: 10 top and bottom right, 30 right, 57 bottom left, 65 top right, 84 right, 85 top, 90 top right, 91 bottom left, 96 top right; Mark Dutka/InHouse: 124 bottom; Michele Dutra/Custom Kitchens by John Wilkins: 41 left; Elliott & Elliott Architects: 92 left; Claudia Fleury/Claudia's Designs: 23 left; Bret Hancock/Thatcher & Thompson Architects: 101 left; Holly Opfelt Design: 69 bottom; Mark Horton: 43 bottom right; House + House Architects: 19 bottom right; Jayne Sanders Interior Design: 93 bottom left; Steve Keating/Designs Northwest Architects: 78 bottom left; Little Folk Art/Susan Salzman: 72 top; Mark Hutker & Associates Architects: 59; Miles Clay Designs: 38 right; Marcia Miller and Steven Stein, Miller/Stein Design: 46 left; Morningstar Marble & Granite: 44 right; Markie Nelson Interior Design: 92 top right; Kevin Patrick O'Brien & Janice Stone Thomas: 41 bottom right, 95 right; Christine Oliver: 97 left; Jim O'Neill/OZ Architects: 46 bottom right; Wendy Nordeck/ Levy Art & Architecture and Sandra Slater/ Environments: 81 bottom; Wayne Palmer: 24 left, 85 bottom; Pamela Pennington Studios: 73 bottom right, 76 right, 80 bottom right, 96 left; Plan One: 80 top; Prentiss Architects: 45 top right; Arne and Sandra Reyier: 47 top right; Heidi Richardson: 36 left; Sagstuen Design: 39 bottom right; Steven W. Sanborn: 95 left; Sandra Bird Custom Kitchens: 36 bottom right; Sant Architects: 43 top right; SkB Architects: 83 top right; Dick Stennick: 8 top left; Henry Taylor: 33; Debra S. Weiss: 69 top, 73 left; Weston & Hewitson Architects: 22 right, 29 bottom right; Henry Wood: 75 top left; Zeff Design: 82 bottom

RETAILERS & MANUFACTURERS

We would like to thank the following retailers and manufacturers for giving us permission to feature their photography: California Closets (© 2005 California Closets Company/All Rights Reserved, each franchise individually owned and operated): 64 left and top right, 65 bottom right, 70 top, 87, 102 left, 103 bottom right; The Container Store: 5 top, 18 right, 26 top, 27 top, 53 middle and bottom right, 55 top, 62 left, 63, 65 bottom left, 68 right, 70 bottom, 98 top left, 99, 100 right; Crate & Barrel/James Baigrie: 19 top right, 90 left; Crate & Barrel/Steven McDonald: 51 top right; Crate & Barrel/Simon Watson: 22 bottom left, 31 bottom right; Crate & Barrel/Gintas Zaranka: 90 bottom; Exposures: 25 right, 91 top right; Frontgate: 49 bottom right, 103 left; Hyloft USA: 107; IKEA: 3 top, 20 top right, 21 all, 30 top left, 38 bottom left, 60 right, 61, 64 bottom right, 68 left, 71 bottom right, 77, 80 bottom left, 91 top left, 93 right, 96 bottom right; Racor, Inc.: 101 right, 102 right; Real Solutions for Real Life: 40 top right, 44 bottom left; Rev-A-Shelf: 55 bottom

index